THE BEGINNING OF DELIVERANCE

TRUE STORY
BOUND. BROKEN. BOUGHT.
DEFEATED. DELIVERED. DAUGHTER.

EVE MATHENY

Princess of the
MOST HIGH KING

Scripture verses are copied from the English Standard Version (ESV), King James Version (KJV), and American Standard Version (ASV) e-sword Bible http://www.e-sword.net

Cover Photo: Stock photo. Posed by model. iStock.com/kevron2001.

Cover Graphic Art Word Design and Placement: Germancreative at Fiverr.

Light Copy-editing: writeralways16 at Fiverr and Zach Naiver.

Published in the United States of America

First Edition Publishing, 2019

Print ISBN: 978-0-692-18985-6

Publisher: Princess of the Most High King, LLC
Email: contact@princessofthemosthighking.com
Website: www.princessofthemosthighking.com

For More Information Contact: Eve Matheny
Email: eve@evematheny.com
Website: www.evematheny.com

"But as for you, ye thought evil against me; but God meant it unto good, to bring to pass, as it is this day, to save much people alive." Genesis 50:20 KJV

"For God so loved the world, that he gave his only begotten Son, that whosoever believeth [G4100] in him should not perish, but have everlasting life." John 3:16 KJV

Strong's G4100 - *pisteuō*

"The KJV translates Strong's G4100 in the following manner: believe (239x), commit unto (4x), commit to (one's) trust (1x), be committed unto (1x), be put in trust with (1x), be commit to one's trust (1x), believer (1x)."[1]

---

[1]
https://www.blueletterbible.org/lang/lexicon/lexicon.cfm?Strongs=G4100&t=KJV

Contents

APPENDICES ARE AVAILABLE AT
WWW.EVEMATHENY.COM

Appendix A - Medical Records
Appendix B - Songs
Appendix C - Unofficial College Transcript
Appendix D - Paralegal Certificate of Completion
Appendix E - Certified Belief Therapist Certificate
Appendix F - Work Performance Evaluations

Acknowledgments

First, I want to thank God for everything! I began writing this book in 2008, and it is now complete. I could not have written and finished this book without You Lord Jesus Christ. I know it is Your story, God. Thank you for allowing me to be a part of Your Kingdom!

I want to thank my family, friends, professors at Wayland Baptist University, and brothers and sisters-in-Christ for your encouragement! I especially want to thank Ken Billings at Wayland Baptist University for offering some needed advice.

I also want to thank Eric Gondwe and his ministry located at http://www.jesuswork.com, as it was this ministry that helped me discover truth about the Bible, truth about deliverance, and most of all truth about Jesus Christ.

I want to thank all of you who have listened to my story and encouraged me in my walk with Jesus Christ! A lot of you, I only know from social media. You have no idea what a difference your kind words and support have made in my life.

I also want to thank all of you who have reached out on YouTube to let me know that my story gave you hope!

Finally, I want to thank every single person who reads and shares this book!

Warnings, Legal Disclaimers, Definitions, and Other Notes

Warnings

I share some details about demonic oppression and possession in this book, so younger children should only read it with their parent's guidance. I went into detail to explain how I fell into such darkness and to demonstrate how various "solutions" failed.

In 2006, I had been diagnosed with schizoaffective disorder (schizophrenia and bipolar disorder), severe anxiety, and severe depression. I had been diagnosed with Attention Deficit Disorder in 2001 and was taking prescribed Adderall for treatment. I eventually became addicted to the Adderall after developing a tolerance to it. I found out recently that Adderall can cause drug-induced schizophrenia. I also had been involved in occult practices before hearing voices. Many people involved in the occult also experience symptoms of schizophrenia or schizoaffective disorder, such as hallucinations and delusions. Therefore, this book touches on both topics.

Legal Disclaimers

I rarely took my medication for schizoaffective disorder, but I do not recommend anyone discontinue medication without first speaking to a healthcare provider. I am not a doctor and do not know the extent of anyone's illness. In 2001, Andrea Yates drowned her five children after discontinuing her medication. She had been hearing voices. Again, I am not a doctor, psychiatrist, psychologist, or a licensed counselor, so I cannot give any medical advice. I am a Certified Belief Therapist through The Therapon Institute, which is a religious credential.

Therefore, I recommend seeking Jesus Christ through prayer and His teachings in one of the first four books (gospels) of the New Testament. If you have trouble concentrating, ask someone you trust to read His teachings to you.

Definitions

Definition of Schizoaffective Disorder.

According to www.mayoclinic.org:

Schizoaffective disorder is a mental disorder in which a person experiences a combination of schizophrenia symptoms, such as hallucinations or delusions, and mood disorder symptoms, such as depression or mania. The two types of schizoaffective disorder both of which include some symptoms

of schizophrenia - are

Bipolar type, which includes episodes of mania and sometimes major depression

Depressive type, which includes only major depressive episodes

Schizoaffective disorder may run a unique course in each affected person, so it's not as well-understood or well-defined as other mental health conditions.

Untreated schizoaffective disorder may lead to problems functioning at work, at school and in social situations, causing loneliness and trouble holding down a job or attending school. People with schizoaffective disorder may need assistance and support with daily functioning. Treatment can help manage symptoms and improve quality of life.

Symptoms

Schizoaffective disorder symptoms may vary from person to person. People with the condition experience psychotic symptoms, such as hallucinations or delusions, as well as symptoms of a mood disorder — either bipolar type (episodes of mania and sometimes depression) or depressive type (episodes of depression).

The course of schizoaffective disorder usually features cycles of severe symptoms followed by periods of improvement with less severe symptoms.

Signs and symptoms of schizoaffective disorder depend on the type — bipolar or depressive type — and may include, among others:

Delusions — having false, fixed beliefs, despite evidence to the contrary

Hallucinations, such as hearing voices or seeing things that aren't there

Symptoms of depression, such as feeling empty, sad or worthless

Periods of manic mood or a sudden increase in energy with behavior that's out of character

Impaired communication, such as only partially answering questions or giving answers that are completely unrelated

Impaired occupational, academic and social functioning

Problems with managing personal care, including cleanliness and physical appearance.[2]

Definition of Deliverance.

According to the www.biblestudy.org:

The term deliverance in religious use describes the process by which a person, believed to be under the control of an evil supernatural entity called a demon, is set free - delivered - from the control of that demon.[3]

According to Eric Gondwe with Jesus Work Ministry, demonic manifestations include:

Body sensations. These include (real and imagined) feelings of movements in the body, tension, heat flow, and pulsation. Other experiences can include out-of-body experiences.

---

[2] http://www.mayoclinic.org/diseases-conditions/schizoaffective disorder/basics/definition/con-20029221

[3] http://www.biblestudy.org/beginner/definition-of-christian-terms/deliverance.html

<u>Visio perceptions</u>. This includes seeing spirit beings that other people cannot see with their ordinary or human sense of sight.

<u>Auditory sensing</u>. This is where one's sense of hearing can hear voices of spirit beings that other people cannot hear with their ordinary or human sense of hearing.

<u>Olfactory Sensing</u>. This is where one's sense of smell can smell odors in an environment that other people cannot smell with their ordinary or human sense of smelling.

<u>Sensing a presence</u>. This is where an individual sense a spirit being is around. Most times they can also say it's hiding, but it's around somewhere. The person may say it's watching everybody's movements, and so on.

Gondwe also states:

The above list is by no means exhaustive. It just outlines the major areas of such spiritual manifestation. Some experience only one or two kinds of manifestations. Others experience more than one. You'll notice that all the above are spiritual experiences beyond our ordinary or earthly senses.

They are supernatural experiences. This is at least where the bible is concerned. The secular world of mental health puts them in the category of psychological disorders. However, these are spiritual matters beyond the mind. Many people experiencing such demonic manifestations are actually intelligent and mentally sound. That's why secular remedies fall short.

Eric Gondwe's Deliverance Ministry Books - Overcoming Demonic Oppression [Emphasis Added][4]

Also, according to www.webmd.com:

Tactile hallucinations - Tactile hallucination is a condition in which it might seem to you that you're being tickled even when no one else is around, or you may have a sense that insects are crawling on or under your skin.[5]

Other Notes

My religious beliefs may be slightly or entirely different from those who assisted in cover design and light copy-editing services. I mention this in case any of you wish to utilize their services.

---

[4] http://www.deliveranceministrybooks.com/html/overcoming-demonic-oppression-book.html
[5] https://www.webmd.com/brain/qa/what-is-tactile-hallucination

Also, this book is a true story, but many names have been changed for privacy reasons.

In addition, to focus on a specific purpose, I chose to keep it short and relevant. Therefore, you will not gain a complete picture of my past. I share specific demonic experiences only to explain how I fell into deception, how the enemy operates, what remedies failed, and how I overcame through the intervention, deliverance, transformation, and grace given by Jesus Christ.

In some of the chapters, I mention that certain people have read a draft of this book prior to it being published. However, they only read the story portion and not the section on "Truths Learned."

Also, I have video testimony on my websites and YouTube channel, but since more detail is offered in this book, I want everyone to be able to have a copy. Therefore, if you cannot afford to purchase an ebook, please send an email to eve@evematheny.com with "Need Free PDF" in the subject line, and I will send you a free PDF.

Lastly, I am working on a second book that shares some of my battles and victories as a Christ-follower that will be helpful for baby Christians. Following Jesus Christ has been exciting, and the battlefield is on an entirely different level! Thank you for reading!

Chapter One
Background

IGNORANCE IS NOT always bliss. We sometimes hear ads, phrases, or jingles that sound good but are not true. Some would even harm us if we didn't already know the "legal disclaimer" to the jingle. For instance, most of us know that we can have a "coke and a smile," but it won't be a healthy one, with our original teeth, if we don't brush and floss regularly due to the sugar and acid content in Coca-Cola.

If anyone had told me that I would go from not believing in demons to thinking I was being tormented by demons shortly before being diagnosed with schizoaffective disorder at the age of 36, I wonder if I would have been more careful about the religious path I was about to take. Would I have wanted to hear the truth, or would I have wanted to stay ignorant?

I am an only child who was born in Utah but raised in Texas. My mother would tell you that I was born independent! I was born premature weighing 5lbs and 3 ounces, but I never had symptoms of schizoaffective disorder until the age of 36. I had some depression in my 20's based on difficult circumstances and was diagnosed with Attention

Deficit Disorder ("ADD") at the age of 29 or 30. As far as I know, neither my parents or grandparents had schizoaffective disorder, severe depression, severe anxiety, or ADD.

I was as emotionally stable as any other child. I loved playing by myself or with friends. I had a great deal of empathy for others. For instance, at the age of 5 and 6, I would cry when certain cartoon characters would get hurt. Even when I took my children to see *The Lion King*, I cried when Simba started blaming himself for his father's death. I know that I cannot be the only adult that cried during that part though! The one big characteristic besides being independent was that I liked to talk, a lot.

I spent most of my younger years singing to my parent's old 45 records, but as soon as I was old enough, I was running in the Texas heat with my friends! I would find locust shells to hook to my shirt just to get a rise out of my mother. I'd also laugh when guzzling down cold milk after playing outside because my mom would have a disgusted look on her face. She still hates milk. The heat didn't bother me, unless I had to run laps in the sun during tennis lessons. I usually got out of it though by asking my coach if I could go lay down in the air-conditioned trailer on the property.

My mom valued manners. She taught me to respect people and answer, "Yes ma'am" and "No ma'am" to elders. She also taught me to think of other people's feelings. She was trying to help me not be self-centered, which was a battle since I was an only child. She also told me to wait until marriage before becoming sexually intimate with someone. We had common arguments over me not wanting to clean my room or what I would wear, like many other mothers and daughters.

I got along well with people at school but did have issues with a boy neighbor on a few occasions. The battle began when I was five or six. He stole my flip flops out of my baby buggy. I chased him, but he then cornered me and held a metal pole to my stomach. Thankfully, one of my shoes slipped out of his hand. When he looked down, I quickly grabbed it and slapped him as hard as I could on one of his arms. He ran home. I never understood why we had issues. However, as I think back, I realize that we never know what someone else is going through. I spent a lot of time with my best friend Dan.

Some of my favorite times were watching my parents sing and dance together. My dad played an acoustic and bass guitar. My mother was a fantastic vocalist. The three of us would sing 60's and 70's songs together occasionally. Other favorite times were camping out on the beach roasting marshmallows and listening to music with my parents, aunts, uncles, and cousins. I still love the beach.

My mom and I spent a lot of time together in the car. She drove me to various classes at different times in my life.

I took roller-skating, tennis, bowling, swimming, Brownies, ballet, tap, jazz, theater, and baton, but not all at the same time. More than anything though, I enjoyed our time together in the car when she would deliver meals to the elderly through the "Meals on Wheels" program. We would discuss how lonely some of the elders were. I was proud of my mom for delivering food and spending time talking with them. It always made me sad thinking someone would feel alone or unloved. It also bothered me a great deal to watch people being bullied.

I got into my first and only girl fight at a slumber party when I was around 10. Kelly scared the birthday girl Kim into believing that a gang of boys were going to come over and hurt us. Kim started crying, so I asked Kelly to shut up. She asked me to make her. Next thing I know we were wrestling in the living room. I have found Dr. Paul Carlin to be right when he says, "A lie is as strong as the truth if a person believes it." Anyway, my mom was called to pick me up.

My family began going to a Catholic church when I was in grade school. I attended Confraternity of Christian Doctrine (CCD) and went through some of the sacraments. I don't remember reading a lot of scripture from the Bible at church. Instead, we read only certain portions that were included in the missalettes used during Mass.

My parents were known and active in the church. They were both in the small choir. My dad played the guitar, and my mom was a vocalist. Everyone loved listening to her sing. I loved the songs about God. Sometimes I would sit directly behind the choir and would look around and watch the congregation. I had heard it was a sin to miss Mass and wondered if God noticed the people who weren't paying attention. I had wondered if He gave them credit. I didn't think credit should be given for only showing up. I was baptized by a priest and received the sacrament of Communion when I was 10 or 11 year's old.

I had believed Jesus Christ existed and that He is the Son of God. I had also classified myself as a Christian. I had heard that He had died for my sins. I didn't understand what all that entailed since I had venial and potential mortal sins that would not be forgiven until I physically made it to a confessional and completed my penance. I was taught that if I committed a mortal sin and died before getting to a physical confessional, I would go to Hell. *What about the disabled? What about people who are too poor to own a car and have no gas money?*

I had believed that God would understand if someone could not physically make it to a church building and that we are able to confess our sins directly to Him. However, I still didn't take communion until confessing my sins to a priest. During confession, the priest would tell me what prayers I needed to say. He also told me how many times to repeat each one. It was usually a combination of "Our Father's" and "Hail Mary's." I was told that after I did penance, my sins would be absolved. However, I stopped regularly going to church when we moved. I was fifteen.

Chapter Two

The Occult

I WAS SIXTEEN when we moved again. This time into a former model home. I had made decent grades at my former school, and I was hoping I'd make good grades at my new one. Everyone was friendly, especially those in my drama class. I met two girls who were also new. The three of us became close friends. I loved reading, music, fashion, and hanging out with my girlfriends. I was a virgin and told every boy that I "went with" that I was waiting for marriage before having sex. I played tennis in junior high and lettered in high school. I was number three on the varsity team. I could never beat two of the other girls.

During those years, my great-grandmother had passed away. My parents had moved some of her old books into what we had called the game room, which was a garage that had been converted into a nice, air-conditioned, carpeted room. One book was on casting spells and another on interpreting dreams. We assumed the books were purchased in bulk at a garage sale.

I had always loved to read, especially Nancy Drew and The Hardy Boys. I also enjoyed reading a college psychology book that I picked up from someone. I was fascinated with the human brain and how it worked, so I was curious about the book on casting spells. When I first opened it, I saw a repulsive goat image, but I kept reading. I couldn't imagine someone wanting something so badly that they would dig up a grave and/or put things in their mouth that were grown out of a dead body. I used the book for a school book report because I thought it was strange, but I had zero interest in spells. I also never liked participating in playing slumber party middle school "games" like Bloody Mary or trying to make others levitate by chanting phrases.

After reading the spell book, weird things began happening in our house and in our cars. Random items would disappear and then reappear. My mother felt someone tap her on the back of her shoulder in the car. I had felt someone touch me on the back of my shoulder in the kitchen. Also, my mom went to take a nap one afternoon and physically felt something pushing her through the mattress. She said it looked like a monster, but she wasn't sure if she had only dreamed about it. On another night, my friend Janice was with me when my skirt disappeared. Because we were going out that night, we cleaned my room looking for it. We picked everything up before we went downstairs to eat. After dinner, we ran upstairs to my room to see the skirt spread out on the carpet. On another day, Janice asked me to pick up one of her friends Tara to take her home. Later Tara told Janice that she sensed an entity riding in the car with us and asked where I lived. Apparently, Tara's dad had walked through our house when it was a model home. He wanted to talk with me. Next thing I know, I'm on the phone talking to Tara's dad who is telling me that we have two entities living in our home; one was an old man, and the other was a girl my age, who was jealous of me. He went on to say that I was experiencing things disappearing and reappearing because I had opened a door by reading the spell book. I tried to block everything out and stay focused on other things, like my social life.

Most of my friends did not have to be home by a certain time, so I began coming home after my curfew because I wanted to stay out with them. Most of the time, I would call my mom and let her know that I was running late, but on those late nights, she would be sitting on the stairs waiting for me to walk in the door. I wish I would have understood how much she loved me and that she wasn't trying to control me.

I also started doing other things like smoking cigarettes. I had never done drugs and was still a virgin, so it was a definite change when I began smoking cigarettes. It was occasional at first, but a few years later I was up to a half-pack a day. Since I was on the varsity tennis team in high school, I wouldn't smoke in the designated smoking area at school for fear that my coach would see me. However, I did smoke a few cigarettes with a girlfriend in a school bathroom, but I didn't like doing that. I mainly did it out of peer pressure.

Some Sundays, I would borrow my parent's station wagon or Monty Carlo and drive my friends around Bear Creek Park to check out the guys because it was the 'thing to do' back then. One Sunday, I locked eyes with Anthony who was standing at a corner in the park. He was tall, dark-haired, green-eyed, clean cut, and well dressed. He smiled, and I smiled right back. I thought it was "love at first sight." He came up to my car window and asked if I would give him a ride to the store to use the pay phone. I agreed to take him. He rode in the back seat of the car. Once we got to the store, he asked me for my phone number. He was a year older than me. He had just moved to Houston from another state so that he could live with his mother. His dad had passed away. He was no longer in high school. He called me that day, and we soon became a couple.

Chapter Three
Nicole, Nadia, and Nick

ANTHONY AND I were together for approximately six months before my daughter Nicole was conceived. I was seventeen years old when sent to a school for pregnant teenagers. I decided to move in with Anthony and his mother. He drove me to and from school. When Nicole was born, I felt a love I had never felt before! Hearing her cry for the first time amazed me. I stayed with Anthony for a while but left due to the way he treated me. I moved back in with my parents.

After having Nicole, I was able to attend my regular high school. I enrolled in a vocational program so that I could learn skills that would help me in a business setting. I began working part-time. I loved the idea of not having to entirely depend on someone. My mom watched Nicole during the day and loved having that time with her!

It wasn't long before I met Hank. Janice had taken me to his house so that she could talk to his brother. I was immediately smitten. We were complete opposites in the way we dressed, musical taste, and our religious beliefs. I had loved pop and industrial dance music, and he listened to death metal like Slayer and King Diamond. Later, we became a couple.

One night, he showed me a satanic bible. He said that Satanism centers around pleasing self, which I thought was strange. He said that's why birthdays are the most important date to Satanists. I understand now that some people who label themselves as Satanists can be agnostic or atheists and do not claim to worship Lucifer. However, some do, so it seems to depend on who you ask.

Later in our relationship, I attended a Flotsam and Jetsam and King Diamond concert with him and approximately five or six of his friends. I was waiting in the front row close to the stage with the guys. Someone had told me that I would not want to be there when the band came out. They said I'd get hurt. I told them I could handle it, but I was wrong. As soon as the first guitar note sounded, I was shoved into a metal bar that separated me from the stage. I couldn't breathe for a few seconds. I then felt someone kicking me in the head with their combat boots. I was thankful when one of Hank's friends pulled me out of the crowd, handed me a grape Blow-Up Pop, and sat down with me on a couch.

We sat and watched young boys and men angrily run around hitting each other yelling "death" and "pain"! These guys were hurting each other for fun, and I didn't understand why. The show became grotesque when King Diamond came on stage. I hated the theatrics. All in all, I have realized that the devil is not in the details. He distorts them. He distorts the truth. Sometimes it is subtle and hard to detect, but it wasn't that night. I broke up with Hank later in our relationship because he told me that he did something horrific. He later told me it was a lie to get attention, but I wasn't sure I believed him.

Months later after smoking marijuana and taking Ecstasy with my friends Sam and Kelly, I decided that I wanted to drop off some of Hank's clothes. I knew that there was a party at his house and that some old friends would be there. Sam and Kelly dropped me off at the party and told me that they would be back. They never showed back up. Once the party started to die down, Hank asked me to talk with him in his mother's room. My second daughter was conceived that night, but I didn't get back with Hank.

Soon after, Anthony asked me to marry him. I told him that I was pregnant with Hank's baby. Anthony said he'd take care of all of us. We married, but I left after a few months due to his treatment of me. He later ended up going to prison.

Later that year, my mom took me to hire a lawyer so that I could get an annulment or file for divorce. The lawyer's legal secretary seemed nice. I remember thinking that I might want to be a legal secretary one day. My legal problems were complicated. Since Nicole had been born before the marriage, she was not legally Anthony's child even though he was her biological father. However, since I married Anthony while I was pregnant with Hank's baby, Anthony was the legal father of Hank's baby. I finally told Hank that I was pregnant. I also told him that I believed it would best to place her for open adoption considering all the circumstances. I wanted her raised in a safe, stable, and healthy environment, and so he reluctantly agreed. It was a difficult decision for both of us. I interviewed a very nice couple and chose them to be the adoptive parents.

During this time, I worked with a lady who was sweet, supportive, and encouraging. I remember her being a Christian. She was different than other people. I wanted to go to church with her, but the company we worked for went out of business and we lost touch. I will never forget her kindness though. She helped me have hope when I was struggling emotionally.

In September, I gave birth to a beautiful baby girl. I was nineteen year's old. Hank came to visit us in the hospital. I didn't want to let her go. Nadia was beautiful. Her adoptive mother was waiting for me to give Nadia to her but then went downstairs to give me some alone time. I knew there was no turning back. I had already signed papers. I was holding Nadia in my arms while my mom or dad wheeled me out of the hospital exit to the adoptive mother's vehicle. I handed the adoptive mother my daughter and felt like a part of me had been ripped out, but I knew she'd give her more than I could.[6] I have never felt such intense emotional pain as I did that day. Today, it is still difficult. I am so thankful that she communicates with me though!

Later in the year, I began seeing my friend Martha's cousin Curt even though he lived about 45 minutes away from me. I had moved into a little one-bedroom apartment that wasn't far from my parent's house. It wasn't long before Curt moved in with me. Not too long after that, my dad accepted a position in San Antonio. Since I had a good job in Houston, I decided to stay. We all came to an agreement that my parents would keep Nicole with them until I got on my feet. I couldn't afford daycare and was hoping for a promotion. I had been working as a Receptionist and Set-Up Clerk for a mortgage company, and I wanted to become a Loan Processor.

Curt and I didn't have a car for a while, so he walked to work. I carpooled with a co-worker who lived in the apartment complex next to me. I was later promoted, and we moved into a two-bedroom apartment in the same complex. Curt's best friend Steve moved in soon after. Steve was in a local rock band, and he came with the lifestyle! Girls and beer.

---

[6] My mom, aunt, Nicole, and I flew to California to meet Nadia when she was nine year's old. Hank and I have spoken a few times within the last ten years, and he has read a draft of this book.

I later broke up with Curt, and he moved out. I was planning on moving to San Antonio to live with my daughter, but right before that Steve and I became involved. Neither one of us had talked about becoming a couple or about the future, and I was determined to move. My employer was allowing me to transfer to their San Antonio office, so I found a small one-bedroom apartment in the same complex as my parents. Nicole moved in with me. She was three years old. I loved being near my family!

Steve visited. During one visit, he asked me to ride to Houston for the weekend, so my mom watched Nicole. It was during that time that our son Nick was conceived. Shortly after, my parents moved back to Houston because my dad had taken a position. I decided to move back with them. As a result, Nicole and I began spending more time with Steve. I quickly rented an apartment for the three of us. My mom watched Nicole while I worked. I gave birth to Nick when I was twenty-two. Nicole was four.

Chapter Four

Is Happiness the Goal in Life?

MY PARENTS LATER moved back to San Antonio so that my dad could start a new job. I later decided to take Nicole and Nick and move to San Antonio, too. I wanted to leave Steve because of our fights and the "rock-n-roll lifestyle," of recreational partying and chaos. I had become good friends with one of Steve's platonic girlfriends, Carrie. She decided to move to San Antonio also, so we became roommates. I helped her get a job working with me at a mortgage company. The four of us lived in a two-bedroom apartment that was less than 10 minutes from work. Nicole was six years old; Nick was two. I was twenty-four.

I soon began dating a Navy guy for a few months, but he had to move due to being in the military. I never thought I'd see him again. His name was Wes. Carrie moved out around that time. Soon after, Steve drove to San Antonio asking me to get back with him, so I let him move in with me. We made some friends in the apartments. Sam, Bobby, and Charlotte. We began to hang out with them on a regular basis, so we became best friends with Sam and Charlotte.

Strange things began happening though. I began having severe sleep paralysis in that apartment. I began reading a book on the paranormal to find an explanation, which seemed to make me feel worse inside. Then one night while lying in bed, I felt like something was hovering over my body. It then felt like something powerful yanked my spirit right out of my body and swung it around in circles over the bed. I could sense the evil. I was able to look down and see my physical body next to Steve's in the bed. It then felt like I was thrown back into my physical body. I was terrified! I continued to suffer from sleep paralysis for years.

However, the kids and I had good times in that apartment even before Steve came back. I used to love it when Nick would have us stand in front of the TV, hold hands, and sing "I Love You," by Barney. He loved Barney. He loved family time. He was an energetic, happy child. Nicole was quieter and extremely observant. She liked to know what we adults were doing, and enjoyed being with us, but she also loved playing outside with her best friend, Sammy. Once Steve moved in, we spent a lot of time barbecuing, swimming, or just hanging out and talking with Sam, Charlotte, and Bobby.

Steve and I went to Mardi Gras in Galveston a couple of times. I remember reading an article while returning home that said that Mardi Gras was a Catholic celebration about indulging before Lent. The article suggested that it was okay to sin before Lent, which I thought was strange. I wasn't a practicing Catholic, but I didn't understand why God would be okay with people ever sinning, before Lent, or after, especially intentionally. I understood that some may overeat a little before fasting, but most of the people that I saw at Mardi Gras were extremely intoxicated, including myself. I still went years after, but always remembered that article.

Later, I ended up leaving the mortgage company to work as a receptionist for a law firm. I was always breaking up with Steve, so there were long periods of time when I was a single mother. Steve had decided to live outside of San Antonio instead of moving back to Houston. Because my parents didn't like me and the kids living in an apartment, they assumed a home for us to live in. I'd was giving my parents money every month to cover the mortgage payments, which were affordable unless I had unexpected expenses come up. The house was modest and cute. It was also located in a cul-de-sac, which I thought was great for the kids!

At various times, we either had season passes to Sea World or Fiesta Texas. The kids would enjoy the water-parks and rides. Sometimes we would sing around the house and take videos of ourselves pretending to be singers from our favorite bands. Nicole and Nick also loved playing video games, but they did spend a good amount of time playing outdoors with the neighborhood kids, too. Most of the time, I was exhausted from work, so McDonald's or Sonic fed them. Deep in my heart, I wanted to do more for them. I felt depleted after the long work days, especially when I had to work overtime.

By the time I reached twenty-seven, my focus had turned to Jesus Christ when I had heard the famous song, "Jesus Freak" by DC Talk. I remember thinking DC Talk was cool for playing a song about loving Jesus. It was refreshing to hear because it was focused on Jesus Christ, not religion. I enjoyed the song so much that I asked my mother if we could go to a Billy Graham event where DC Talk would be playing. I had no idea who Billy Graham was, but we went. We both enjoyed it. I remember when Billy Graham asked if we wanted to give our lives to Jesus Christ (I'm not sure if he phrased it that way verbatim), I didn't hesitate to get out of my chair and walk down the aisle believing that I was giving my life to Christ. I did not seek Jesus Christ through His teachings in the Bible, or even read the Bible. I had thought that something would change in my life from just walking down the aisle, but it didn't, at least not then.

Steve and I got back together at some point, but I broke up with him for good in 1999, at the age of twenty-nine.[7] After my breakup with Steve, I was tested for Attention Deficit Disorder (ADD) and was prescribed Adderall. It seemed to help me focus and have more motivation, which in

---

[7] Steve and I have both moved on with our lives, but we do 'check in' with each other occasionally to see how everyone is doing.

turn seemed to help with single motherhood, having to work late, and everything else.

If I cooked, it was enchiladas, tuna with noodles, or pork chops and rice. My children still like to playfully tease me about the bloody and burnt chicken and burned fries I once made. However, I would often drive through a fast food restaurant, order pizza, or they would eat something that did not need to be cooked.

We didn't have much money. Anthony was never required to pay child support, and even if he had been, he could not help us because he was in prison most of the time. However, at one point I began receiving $256.00 a month from Steve, which helped with after school daycare expenses. I played with the kids as much as I physically could. Many times, there was a fine line between 'mother' and 'friend' though. It was hard discipling them. I was not good at it.

One night I thought about a letter that Wes had sent to my mom's house years before to see if I was still with Steve. I decided to reach out to him to see how he was doing. We were married two years later, so Nicole and Nick became Wes's step-children.

Wes helped stabilize the home environment and motivated me to go back to college (I had tried before, but it didn't work out). He was in graduate school studying biochemistry during our marriage. He was receiving a stipend, which along with my income helped us financially.

He had been in 3rd FORECON. His military background added structure to the household.

We spent most of our time working out, watching X-Files, and playing video games. We would take Nicole and Nick out of school when a new Harry Potter movie came out. I remember that Nick's best friend's mom wouldn't let her son watch Harry Potter because they were Christians. I didn't understand why reading or watching Harry Potter was a problem. "It was a just a movie," I thought, but I respected her decision.[8]

Later, Nick understandably wanted to live with his dad, for once, since he only saw him on weekends and during the Summer. We all wanted him to stay, but I understood that the court would allow him to have a say. It was difficult to adjust. I struggled emotionally knowing that I was only going to see him on certain weekends and only for a short time during the Summer.

After that, I had to work long hours as a Paralegal for a Plaintiff attorney. It had felt as though my job was harming my marriage. I was tired when I got home. Since I had always

---

[8] Today, I know some Christians who do watch it, but I don't. I also remember watching the movie *The Craft* and it having a significant influence on me. I had an attraction to the occult but had not dabbled much. I had consulted fortune tellers before, and I played with a Ouija board a few times with Steve, but we had a strange and scary experience when one of our bedroom doors slammed shut while we were playing. We threw the board in a garbage dumpster and never used one again.

wanted to be an entrepreneur and ran across an opportunity to sell legal plans, a product I firmly believed in, I did the "not so smart" thing and just quit my job, without consulting Wes. So, as I started my own business, my marriage was ending. I had threatened divorce many times because I felt like we were becoming further apart. Wes moved out and decided to file for divorce. I was thirty-five with a thirteen-year-old and a seventeen-year-old. Nick was still living with his dad.

Since we had no money, I sold a lot of our furnishings to pay bills and accumulate a little money to invest in my business of selling prepaid legal plans. I was offering it to individuals and businesses. I also took special training classes so that I could sell it to companies who wanted to offer it to their employees as a benefit. I saw the value and was excited about people being able to use the services.

However, I was depressed about the divorce. I had such big dreams but was broke. Oddly, it was during this time that Nicole and I signed up as volunteers to help children at the SAMM Ministries Transitional Shelter.[9] We used the shelter's curriculum to help children develop life skills. It was good for me and Nicole to do something good together. We both loved those kids. Unfortunately, we had to stop due to my life becoming unbalanced.

---

[9] https://www.samm.org/learn/how-we-help/traditional-housing/

I had begun abusing the Adderall a little because it would wear off early leaving me feeling tired and unmotivated. For the most part, any time that I was awake, I was on Adderall. I felt like I needed it to be a better mother, business owner, house-cleaner, and friend. Plus, my psychiatrist felt like I needed it, and I agreed.

I thought it was a supplement to help me function like normal women. In my eyes, most women seemed to be like superwoman compared to me. I was lethargic and unmotivated without it, and sadly I wasn't even close to superwoman with it. I was just trying to survive with the goal of meeting the status quo, which seemed impossible. I would have loved to finish college but could never stick with it. Between financial issues, workload, kids, and my energy level, it wasn't happening. I sadly accepted that I was not an accomplished woman. I hadn't even finished Paralegal school to get my certificate due to a financial issue, and I only had one more semester.

Unlike many people in sales, money did not drive me. I didn't have this huge desire for material things but would *try* to have that desire hoping that it would fuel me into wanting to sell more plans. Of course, I did need and want to earn money to pay bills, but I didn't want "stuff" bad enough. The motivation came from it being a good product that would help others. I stayed depressed and asked myself if being happy was the purpose of life. At that time, I thought it was. So, I tried to find out what would make me happy. I later decided that the only way to be happy was to have everything that I wanted, or to fulfill my life purpose. I wrote this journal entry:

> My purpose: leader & help other[s] find economic freedom through positive thoughts & God & faith. To counsel. To write books. To fund Nick & [Nicole's] dreams. To be a positive influence on everyone's lives. To help them see the good & the power they have in themselves. I want to change people's lives for the better & I've got to start w/mine.

I wanted to accomplish this by being a motivational speaker, but first I knew that I needed to motivate myself.

Chapter Five
New Age Path

I DECIDED TO become a "spiritual" positive person who would work on having a very close spiritual relationship with Jesus Christ. I never read the Holy Bible. I did not personally know Jesus Christ, but I *felt* like God was with me, sometimes. Of course, *feeling* something doesn't make it true, but back then I went by my feelings. I thought I was basically a good person. I believed in Jesus Christ's existence and had heard that He died for my sins. I didn't understand everything though. I didn't know His teachings. I didn't know much about Him.

Because I was broke, I began meditating and reading all the self-help books that I could get my hands on. I read books telling me how to get what I want. These books were telling me to expect that I would receive whatever I asked by a supernatural force, which was alleged to be God. Now I had thought this was the God in the Bible that I heard about in church. However, because I didn't read the Bible, I had no spiritual discernment to understand the difference between God's character vs. what the metaphysical world (new age world) was teaching me.

One of the first books that introduced me to the new age doctrine was *The Secret* by Rhonda Byrne.[10] I also had

---

[10] There are claims that the doctrine in *The Secret* comes from a woman, Esther Hicks, who channels an entity who calls itself Abraham Hicks (who claims to be a "we"). The teachings are based on the Law of Attraction. I do not recommend reading anything about the Law of Attraction, the book *The Secret,* or listening to the advice given through Esther Hicks. I'm only providing a web address to show that I'm telling the truth. http://www.allaboutprosperity.com/abraham-hicks the secret-behind the-secret-full-movie/

Also, a link to *The Secret's 10th Anniversary Edition* acknowledges the "inspirational teachings" of "Jerry and Esther Hicks and the teachings of Abraham." https://books.google.com/books/about/The_Secret.html?id=MagHtB5NKVcC&printsec=frontcover&source=kp_read_button#v=onepage&q&f=false

In addition, *The Secret* references scripture. Specifically, on receiving what you ask for from God. *The Secret* calls God "the universe," which is not the biblical God who created all humanity and who wants a relationship with us. *The Secret* takes Jesus Christ's teachings out of context and asks people to pray to another "god" a/k/a "the universe." Also, God is not going to give us something that does not line up with His doctrine and will. Further, Jesus Christ told His disciples, *"When ye pray, say, Our Father which art in heaven, Hallowed be thy name. Thy kingdom come. Thy will be done, as in heaven, so in earth. Give us day by day our daily bread. And forgive us our sins; for we also forgive every one that is indebted to us. And lead us not into temptation; but deliver us from evil."* Luke 11:2-4 KJV. God is not a "genie in a bottle," and He's not here to grant sinful wishes; Jesus Christ came to deliver us from sin and help us be free from it, which is amazing! He's not going to answer prayers that are asked to be fulfilled by something He created, such as the universe.

Many occult related doctrine will use biblical scripture or Jesus Christ's name, but their doctrine will 1. twist truth making the doctrine false; 2. omit truth so a person cannot see the whole picture; and, 3. oppose some or all New Testament teachings.

For example, you may have heard of the "prosperity gospel." Much of that "gospel" sounds a lot like the doctrine in *The Secret*. Years ago, I had noticed that the doctrine of Lakewood Church sounded like the doctrine in *The Secret*. It may still today. I haven't listened to Joel the DVD. I began preaching it to Nicole, but she wasn't interested, which was good. I had received the DVD from salespeople involved in my business. It was suggested that I use it as a tool to motivate myself and my team. I trusted the philosophy and didn't question anything. This book is popular. Oprah Winfrey has promoted it.

The basic premise of *The Secret* is self-rule and treating a "god" the "universe" like a 'genie in a bottle' to answer prayers. Supposedly, people who practiced *The Secret* found the key to success. Well, since I hadn't been very successful, I began doing everything that I was taught. According to many books, the key to life was being "happy" and "fulfilled," and the only way to be happy is to live your life the way that you want.

Osteen much, but I have heard that he does not talk about sin or Hell or following Jesus Christ instead of self. If that is true, then those are red flags. Also, I had noticed that Oprah Winfrey had rejected Jesus Christ as Lord, has promoted *The Secret*, and has also attended Lakewood Church. https://www.nytimes.com/2008/04/26/arts/26secr.html

Also, in many prosperity gospel churches the worship bands may create music that seems to hold sound doctrine, or the songs are vague and could be talking about Jesus Christ, but when we hear the pastors' doctrine, or look at the books the pastor promotes, we can see false doctrine that turns people away from the truth, which means turning people away from finding freedom from all kinds of sickness and spiritual death. It can be hard to discern. If a church doesn't talk about Jesus Christ being God and exalt Him over us, doesn't talk about sin, doesn't talk about repenting of sin, and doesn't talk about following Jesus Christ and make Him the center, then something is wrong. In addition, in speaking about false teachers, Jesus said, *"Ye shall know them by their fruits..."* Matthew 7:16 KJV

I later began to read similar types of books, which also included connecting my mind and spirit with people in the physical realm and spirit guides in the spiritual realm. I started venturing out into new territory and imposing my will onto other people with my mind. I did this while meditating (transcendental) on Adderall, which is made of amphetamine salts, a Schedule II controlled substance, which in my opinion is as strong as cocaine. I found out much later that occult involvement and Adderall have been known to cause symptoms of schizophrenia.[11]

Most of the books that I had been reading did not talk about that Spiritual Force being God from the Bible, but I was deceiving myself believing that our Creator was the same God that everyone worshiped and that we all had different ways of worshiping Him. Since I began to have more free time during the day, I started spending more time meditating, praying to the "universe," and reading Ann Rice books.

I had always had a fascination with vampires, so I loved her books. I had even fantasized about being a vampire,

---

[11] Adderall is a Schedule II controlled substance.
https://www.addictioncenter.com/addiction/controlled-substances-act-and-scheduling/
Adderall can cause drug-induced schizoaffective disorder.
https://www.therecoveryvillage.com/adderalladdiction/adderall-causes-psychosis-schizophrenia/
Occult practices have been known to cause some people to have symptoms of schizoaffective disorder. One source can be found at
http://www.womenofgrace.com/blog/?p=13386

so that I could look young, be powerful, and live forever. I remember reading one of Rice's books *Memnoch the Devil* that made it appear as though Satan was the "cool one" and God was the "bad guy." However, with all the metaphysical books I had been reading, I was starting to believe that God was the "cool one" who wanted me to have everything that I wanted and desired without any boundaries. So, I drank my coffee, contacted my prospects some mornings, earned enough money to barely get by, and began meditating a few hours a night by visualizing my dreams.

I began meditating on material objects like a house, boat, or car. I was trying to desire these things because I didn't know what else would make me happy, other than my children having "stuff," as well. What else was there to fill that void? Nothing else was filling it. I thought all these things would make me and my children happy. Also, I thought that God was with me and that was good enough for me. I was optimistic about my future because I had faith in myself!

Chapter Six

Stuck

I DIDN'T ENJOY being broke, so I found a full-time job working as a Legal Secretary. This was close to the time that I met John in 2006, four months after my divorce. After telling each other that we loved each other, and after he asked me what I would be like if I were his wife, I was abruptly caught off guard when I found out he was married.

He had downed more than a few Budweiser's when he started complaining that Dina was using his debit card. I knew Dina was the mother of his youngest daughter, but I did not think they were married. I just said, "Whoa, wait a minute. Are you still married to her?" His reply, "Well yes, I'm not going to lie to you about it." He then gave me his version of their separation from each other. She allegedly cheated on him while they were living in Houston. He transferred to San Antonio alone and called it a separation. I had thought he was single because he had no wedding band, and his MySpace page indicated that he was a single man. I was devastated, angry, hurt, bitter, and felt incredibly betrayed. I left in the middle of the night. I saw him on a few other occasions but kept breaking it off.

However, I would start missing him and call and ask him if I could see him. He reminded me that I left him and that I "do it all the time." He said he would give me another chance though. I promised him that I wouldn't leave again. It was sad. I was losing all self-respect and self-worth knowing that what I was doing was wrong.

The behavior was not "the me" that I had known in the past. I continued meditating and focusing on my desires, which began to include being in a relationship with John. I had started to see visions me and John having a picnic in the park or dancing. The visions *seemed* beautiful and right, so I would open myself up to the "universe," asking it to give me what I wanted.

I started going out to dance clubs on the weekends with a close friend. I had even bought two hits of Ecstasy and cut them into fourths so that I could take a little bit here and there. I was trying to forget John and be happy due to the moral dilemma, but no matter how many men talked to me, I still felt a dark cloud hanging over my head engulfing and swallowing me up. I couldn't fight it on my own. It was way more powerful than me.

I tried to remind myself to not contact him. I would stalk his MySpace page and see that he was depressed by the things he would write. I then started looking at his wife's

MySpace page. I would sit and read her posts and feel incredible guilt.

I remember lying in my bed one day and feeling a dark, heavy, and furious presence hovering over me. I could feel the intensity of its anger glaring at me. It seemed to be staring right at me. It felt like it was on top of me as if its face was right up against my face. It lingered for a while. I sensed a lot of evil and became frightened, so I pulled my blankets over my head and hoped it would go away.

There was no doubt that something very evil was in my room. I thought back to how I had heard an inner scream once telling me to get the heck out of John's apartment one night and wondered if it had anything to do with this presence. I had never felt anything so intense, especially from something that I could not see. I had a gut feeling that this very presence had a lot to do with my attachment to John and why I felt so controlled when contacting him. I felt like it wasn't really me contacting him. It had begun to feel like something was trying to make me do it. I thought I was possessed. That was the only explanation for this and for everything else that was about to happen.

Meditating and abusing Adderall were making things worse. My head began to feel heavy. I felt drugged even when waking up sober. Plus, Adderall had never made me feel like that. I did not understand what was happening, but I was sure it had something to do with me trying to will away someone's husband with my thoughts. The deception was that the visions that I would see looked nice, so it seemed righteous, but it wasn't because God would not approve of adultery. So, the visions were not from God, but I was double-minded; conflicted.

Even worse, I began hearing a voice who claimed to be John and sounded like John. He would remind me of all these things that we did together. He would tell me that he could listen to my thoughts and that we could communicate like this. This entity could hear any thought that I had. I didn't have to open my mouth to speak. Conversations would go on in my mind all night long. I could hear his thoughts in my head and his voice externally coming from the air. It was like having a conversation with a person physically present. A lot of interaction, laughing about good times together. He apologized for lying. He would tell me that he was beside me on my bed. I didn't know what to think. How did this voice know specific details about John that I would have never remembered? How did this voice know a lot about me and my kids? Sometimes when the voice would say something off the wall, I was sure it was John. It seemed pure and true, but it was a deceiver.

At home one day, I heard what I will call "John's voice" coming from the living room stereo. I was stunned and froze.

The voice was saying how sorry he was for not calling or texting me back. It appeared as though John's thoughts were being made known to me through my stereo.

Also, several nights I heard, "She loves me, and I love her!" Then I would hear a female voice break down crying and saying, "You don't love her. You lust her!" At first, I thought I left on the television, but then I knew something crazy was going on. I also started hearing, "I love you so much." I would hear that voice from an external position, but it didn't sound anything like John's voice. It was a deep voice. Later, I began hearing more voices coming from the living room stereo. Most of the time though, I'd hear voices that seemed to be in the air. It was as invisible people were all around me speaking loudly. In addition, the depression was getting worse. I wrote two journal entries:

> Something is seriously wrong with me right now. I've fallen into a deep depression that I can't seem to snap myself out of it. I know taking Adderall is not helping and I need to figure out a way to safely get off of it. Strange things and sensations are happening.

> Gotta break this trance I'm in; this obsession that sickens me so much. It consumes all other thoughts making them disappear as soon as they're realized. To focus on anything else is the most difficult task – it's like drowning in thick

mud looking for a way out, but you get so lost you forgot there is anything else, much less a way out. You may break out for a little while, but you're sucked back in when you close your eyes to sleep. You wake up in a trance again. You feel controlled, but that's impossible, right? It's like a gravitational force that you fight every second of every day because you know if you stay there too long you'll never come back up.

Chapter Seven

Who Can Save Me?

FEELING BETTER ONE morning, I picked up breakfast. As I walked in my house towards my computer, I heard a loud and intense voice coming from the stereo saying, "You are so sexy!" I was so startled that I dropped my orange juice spilling it all over the floor. I broke down crying.

That was not the sweet voice I had been talking with at night. Also, I was still hearing, "I love you so much" ten to fifteen times a day. I was also having trouble hearing my friends while using my cell phone because of the voices. I couldn't understand why this was happening to me. Sometimes I would hear a voice tell me that God was with me. I hoped that to be true, but it didn't feel like it. *Maybe my house was haunted*, I thought, but I had lived there 11 years and never had issues. Then I remembered how I'd hear voices at work, also. *Maybe I was haunted.*

Most of the voices I'd hear at work were what I would call "good voices." They would tell me when to drink some water and when to eat. I wasn't drinking or eating much; I'd forget. They would tell me that I was doing a good job. They would tell me that my boss was nice and that my parents loved me. They would tell me to stop smoking and to stay away from drugs. These voices said that they were angels, and after hearing the deep scary voice coming from my stereo, I was relieved to know that I could hear some "good voices." I began to trust them.

Another day after walking in the door after work, I heard a loud voice from the stereo say, "I can see you." "I can see you." Before long, I was always hearing that this entity could see me. He would comment on what I was wearing and where I was located in the house. Some early mornings, I would smell sulfur, and my eyes burned.

During that time, only two people knew that something was going on with me; my best friend Shelly and my daughter Nicole. Shelly didn't know much though. Since Nicole lived with me, she witnessed a lot of my fear and hysteria. I couldn't hide what was going on, and I didn't want her to worry, but I knew I had to get help fast.

I first decided to go see a psychic who operated her business around the corner. She said she needed $1,500.00 to perform an exorcism because the demon over my head feared her but strong. She explained that her fee was high because of the risk of putting her family in danger. I didn't have $1,500.00. Since I was raised Roman Catholic, she said that I could get a free exorcism from the church. She gave me one white and one red candle. She told me to burn the white candle first and then the red one (this made things worse). She gave me something to put over the front door of the house. I gave her my last $60.00 and thanked her.

I drove home and lit the white candle immediately. Shortly after that, I was told by a voice that Nicole would be next. Hearing that tore me up inside. I could not handle what was happening. I could not control it. I could not escape it. Earlier, I even thought I had seen our dining room table shake. I was going insane. There was no peace. Even worse, I could not protect Nicole.

Because I was scared, I woke Nicole up from a nap and told her everything. I was a mess and didn't realize that my being upset and frantic was making things worse for her. All I wanted to do was get her out of that house. I told her that we had to get out right then and that she could not stay. I told her that we needed to find a priest as soon as possible. I didn't have any protection. I could not protect myself, much less my 18-year-old daughter.

Also, I would space out sometimes when Nicole would talk because the voices were louder than her voice. They were also telling me to get my dog out of the house. There were also voices having conversations with each other, which made it difficult to make out who was saying what.

I finally got Nicole in the car and then broke down crying. She immediately assumed it was a mental illness, and not anything supernatural or spiritual, because she could not hear the voices and she didn't see the table shake inside the house. We went to a church, but there was no priest available. I eventually found a priest at another church who referred me to the only church in San Antonio that would perform exorcisms; St. Mary Magdalene. I didn't know where it was located, but I didn't have any gas money, so I knew that I wouldn't be able to get there that day. I was terrified to go back home. I could hear laughing and a voice was telling me that he was poking holes in my feet while I was sitting in the car with Nicole. There was no escape. I had no power to stop it. *The police could not save me. My parents could not save me. My boss could not save me. I could not save me. No one on Earth could save me. I had no control.* This wasn't just about hearing voices. I could feel pain in my feet. It felt as if sharp fingernails were being driven in the bottom of my feet while a voice told me that he was drinking my blood. I felt tortured. This became a frequent occurrence.

I started complaining about the pain and told Nicole what the voice was saying, against my better judgment. Then Nicole and I started fighting. I drove around for a while and then decided to go home. I was scared and felt helpless. It was one thing to mess with me, but to threaten to mess with my daughter was fueling a stronger desire for immediate help. I had no idea that this was going to get worse. I wrote this my journal:

I heard a second voice that chilled every bone in my body. The voice was loud, clear, not too deep, but I knew it... I can't believe this is happening to me.

It wasn't long before I heard another voice. I'll call it, "Dina." Her voice was very loud and angry. I could feel someone's breath on my face while hearing this voice scream, "You stole my husband from me, you ...! I'm going to kick your...!" "You don't know who you are messing with!" I could hear this voice over my kids, over the voices of people standing around me at work, and over the music on the radio. Dina's voice would scream at me on a regular basis. I would also smell baby lotion. She would ask if I could smell her and John's baby girl. Most of the time she would constantly remind me that I didn't know who I was messing with.

Chapter Eight
Wilderness of Madness

IT WAS BEGINNING to get late. The white candle had nearly burned all the way down, so it was time to light the red one. I had no idea what this meant or what I was doing, but it made things worse. To try to get some rest that night, I had taken a few Benadryl, but that did not help. I was about to experience a horrible night.

There was so much going on at one time. The voices never stopped. Ever. It was constant, and there were many. Different pitches and tones. There was not a moment's peace. I was still being reminded that I didn't know who I was messing with, and Dina's voice would still ring loudly in my ears calling me names and threatening me. I then began hearing John's voice fighting with Dina, accompanied by sharp sensations that would begin in my feet and then move up and throughout my body. The fights between John and Dina were terrible. I heard all kinds of things that I did not want to hear. Later, I was introduced to a new loud and scary voice.

I was sitting on my bed listening to John and Dina fight (I had no choice but to listen) when I heard a loud male voice yell at me, as if he were close to my face, "John Marshall is a loser!" "How can you possibly love him?" "Why would you even want him?" I immediately asked who he was. I had a sense of dread about this one. He said his name was Larry and that he was a demon. I asked him where he was. He said that he was sitting beside me on the bed. He asked if I wanted him to show himself to me. I said, "No!" I jumped off my bed and started walking towards the living area and began feeling swirling energy move around my feet. I could hear his laughter. He enjoyed my fear. I thought about that fact for a while. He went on to tell me that there were many demons inside of me. I finally realized there was no escape. I could not get away, so I went back to my room and laid down on my bed.

It began to feel like a cover of darkness was slowly being laid over me. The red candle was still burning on my nightstand. It was the only light in the room. My mind began to slow down. My thoughts were in slow motion, and I had no control over this. *What was about to happen to me*, I thought. I felt hypnotized and severely drugged. I wasn't taking any drugs or my prescribed Adderall, only Benadryl. I could hear my own cell phone voicemail recording coming out of my bedroom radio speaker saying, "I'm not available right now, but if you leave a message, I'll call you right back." It was so loud, and it was MY voice. They could imitate my voice perfectly. Then the interrogations started. I wrote a journal entry about this:

> I feel like someone else has complete control over my mind – pushing buttons to elicit the strongest and most unbearable emotional distress - - block the connection; what is happening to me? I'm being influenced and controlled.

I was asked all kinds of questions. "Would you marry John? Would you marry John if he were a criminal? Would you help take care of his two children? How would you deal with Dina? Do you really think that Dina would accept you as the step-mother of her child?" Then I'd hear another voice that sounded like John say, "What did she say?" I'd then hear someone tell him what I had thought. Then I'd hear the voice that sounded like John say, "I can't keep doing this to her, I just can't," but the questions continued. A lot of them were asked by the voice claiming to be Dina. "Would you stay married to John if he cheated on you? Would you marry him right now if you could? I tried not to answer the questions, but I would think about how I would respond, and these entities could hear my thoughts. Then Dina would tell me that she loved John, and I would smell baby lotion again while hearing her scream, "Can you smell that? That is our baby girl after taking a bath!" Dina and John would then argue.

I couldn't pull myself up. I felt so drugged. My mind felt like something powerful was controlling it. Everything was in slow motion. The voices were slow and thick. They demanded answers to all their questions. Again, I began to respond and answer their questions with my thoughts. Worse, my brain and skin began to feel like they were on fire. It sounded and smelled like I was being cooked. I could hear horrible crackling and sizzling noises coming from my head. The intense burning in my arms and intense sensations in my feet began moving up and throughout my body. These sensations had occurred on a regular basis but were worse this night.

I was dizzy and felt hypnotized. I could hear different kinds of evil chanting throughout the night. I tried not to focus on the words. I had wished that I could sit up and blow out the red candle. I could still hear Dina and John fighting. Then Larry told me that John and Dina could not only hear my voice but could hear Larry's, as well. He asked me why I had kept going back to John after finding out that he was married. I would answer with my thoughts (because I was trying not to speak at all), and then I'd **hear my voice** tell John and Dina **almost** the truth of what I had thought. The strange thing was my words were twisted around.

For instance, in my thoughts, I was saying that I loved John. I would hear Larry tell John and Dina that he would let them listen to me, but then I would hear my own voice say, "I don't love John." "I never loved John." Listening to my own voice say that when I thought something completely different was messing with my head. Also, if I had a certain thought in my head, or verbalized certain thoughts out loud, such as "I love God," I'd hear my own voice override that and say, "I love Satan," at the same time. This worried me because I would *hear* my own voice say that I loved Satan and invite demons to come over. *Something was trying to control how I thought and using the sound of my voice to do it.* Listening to my own voice changing words, and believing that God, John, and Dina could hear it, brought on much anxiety and severe distress.

Also, my voice could be heard from any area in the house. Most of what I thought was twisted around. I began yelling out loud protesting, "I didn't say that."

I must have been asked 50 or more questions that night and all my answers were mixed with lies. I could hear my voice telling John and Dina those lies. When I would start to protest about the lies to Larry, he would command that I remain quiet. He said that he was trying to help me, and that he loved me, which I thought was ridiculous because he was a demon, and demons can't love.

I then heard Larry tell John that he could only choose one of us and that whoever he didn't pick, Larry was going to take to Hell with him. This went on for a long time. John would choose me then Dina would scream for help and John would change his mind. Then he would select Dina. I would hear my voice scream - I wasn't really screaming – I didn't really believe I was going to Hell then, but I knew that I never wanted to go because it had to be much worse than what was already happening.

I knew Larry was playing some massive mind games. I would hear my voice get in arguments with Dina's voice then I'd listen to her say, "I didn't really say that." So, Dina's "voice" seemed upset that she was hearing her voice telling me lies. Dina would then question me about my love for John again. She would tell me to marry him right now. Then she'd start our wedding vows for us. She asked John if he would, "take this woman to be his lawfully wedded wife..." and he would say, "yes," then she would change her mind and decide that she didn't want me to marry John. All the sudden everything got quiet. Then I heard what I had believed were angels telling the other voices to be quiet and to let me sleep for the night. I heard John say, "I love you." Then I heard what I thought were the angels again quietly tell John to let me sleep. I was happy to be able to sleep. Sometimes I would hear another voice to the left of my ear tell me that John loves me very much but was not yet ready to let go of Dina. I could feel this entity breathe on my left cheek every time he spoke. God would not approve of trying to take someone's husband. God also wouldn't use deception or witchcraft. I believe this voice was a deceiver wrapped up in what *seems* nice or sweet, but God's Word shows God's character.

Sometimes, it seemed like the good and evil voices came out of this entity's mouth. I would feel his or her breath along with the intensity of each voices' words that were spoken. For instance, I would hear Dina through this entity. The breath that I would feel on my face when she spoke was powerful and hit my face hard. Some of the voices were soft and would tell me to focus on God and know that God was with me; to just have faith in God. I had so much faith in God's existence. I just knew that He was going to save me one day. I remember hearing voices one-night singing, "Jesus loves me, yes I know. For the Bible tells me so."

Chapter Nine
Minor Exorcism

I MADE IT to work the next morning, but the voices were loud. I think the night before was the only time they had ever let me rest for a few hours. There was hope. This was far from being over though. I had called and spoke to someone at the Roman Catholic Church and was told that the church could not perform a full exorcism without permission from the Bishop, which would take up to six months. I was to go to attend mass every Sunday, go to confession, and receive Holy Communion. I also needed to have mental illness ruled out before the Bishop would decide. I didn't agree with having mental illness ruled out because I felt it was a spiritual problem, but I attend a few masses, went to confession, and received communion. Sometimes I would hear a voice praying next to me in church, as I did at home.

I was doing terrible physically. I was shaking a lot and frequently cold. I could feel energy moving in and out of me that would chill my bones. I was exhausted. I didn't hardly eat or drink. I forgot about it. I'd hear the voices all day long at work and began talking back to them. I couldn't work well because of the voices and because I had severe anxiety. Sometimes it would take over ten minutes to place an envelope in the printer. My hands would shake, and I felt uncomfortable in my own skin.

One time I heard a voice instruct me to tell my non-messianic Jewish boss that Jesus Christ did exist. My boss already knew my beliefs, and I knew his. I did not follow the voice's instructions. I also understand that was Satan trying to make me start trouble with my boss. It would have looked bad being that I was not right in my mind. I bet the enemy does that a lot to try to make people who claim to be a Christian look bad.

On a work break, I went outside to smoke a cigarette. I heard a voice tell me to jump off the balcony. I realized that I had to get to the church that performed exorcisms as soon as possible! I left a message asking the priest if he could visit with me after I got off work. At the end of the workday, I drove to a parking lot and waited for the priest to call me back. I could barely drive. The voices were telling me that I'd better not see the priest and go to that church. They said they were going to keep me from getting there.

The priest finally called to let me know he would meet with me. The voices were so loud and distracting that it took an hour just to figure out that I had been driving around in circles. I kept recognizing the same streets that I had already passed. The enemy likes to keep people in a wilderness of lies and deception, which prevent a person in bondage from walking outside of the circle of madness. Your thoughts go in circles like a mad dog chasing his or her tail. I prayed for God to please help me find the church. I eventually made it and found the priest that I had talked to over the phone. He took me into a little room. I told him everything that was happening to me. The priest said that by meditating under severe distress and without God's protection, I had opened a door and invited demons in. I agreed, and I still felt that the "mental illness" was a spiritual problem, like the priest said, "demons I had invited in." He said that he could perform a minor exorcism though.

The priest took me into a chapel, anointed my forehead with oil, and held a crucifix against it. He then began praying. I only heard one voice throughout this whole ordeal saying that if I did not stop the priest, the entity would snap my "... neck." This was constantly repeated. I felt like I was in a trance. The priest had done all he could, but nothing changed. The priest gave me a book that I never read because the dog I had been watching for a friend tore it up when I got home. He said it was about a woman who went through the same thing and pulled through. The priest went on to tell me that sometimes these things happen to Christians because God has a special plan for their lives, and He wants them to serve His purpose. It almost seemed like the priest was telling me that this was some kind of test. The priest handed me a Bible, and he blessed a crucifix for me to take home.

Additionally, he handed me some papers containing prayers to say every night to fight curses, witchcraft, and demons. He told me to say my rosary every night and to mention Mary's name. He said that demons hate it when you mention Mary. I had a rosary already, so I thanked him for his time and went home. At some point, I had obtained holy water from a Catholic store, too. I thought I had some ammunition, but things got worse.

Chapter Ten
Fighting Back. Another Round Lost.

I DROVE A black Sebring convertible. I remember putting the top down even when it was 40 degrees outside because the demon complained about the cold. He would tell me that I was starting to make him mad (not in those words) and to put the top up. I became furious and started talking back and doing everything that I knew would upset him. I was hoping he would get sick of it and leave. I handled this the wrong way. I brought on even more harassment by behaving this way and fighting a battle that was not mine to fight.

Things were getting more bizarre, so I had this idea to try to record what was going on in the house, but when I turned on my tape cassette recorder, it busted and left a burnt smell in the air. Also, there seemed to be pockets of cool air in my room. I had believed those were portals for aliens to travel. At times, I could hear two people having a conversation inside my stomach, and it felt like transmitters were running up and down my legs. Also, I would listen to my thoughts accelerate, slow down, and then return to an average rate. I could also feel entities playing with my hair.

Also, I once heard a voice tell me that my maternal grandmother was going to die and that I was going to be Satan's bride.[12] I also heard my mom's voice yell at me. I was still learning that demons can imitate anyone's voice. They also have a lot of knowledge about our lives and families, but they lie and try to reel people in with half-truths, so that they can gain some control over people's thoughts. This type of behavior is also carried out in the physical realm through the deceptive behavior and words of people and deceptive philosophies.

Out of desperation, I began going through every single prayer the priest gave me. I would hear voices cussing, complaining, telling me to stop, and saying, "She's talking about us, let's go," but they would never leave. After reading every single prayer the priest gave me, I would begin to pray the rosary. I would always hear, "Not again!" "Jesus Christ!" This was the first time that it had occurred to me that people say, "Jesus Christ" as a curse word, just like these demons. They didn't curse anyone else. Neither does Hollywood when making movies. I assume His name is used because Jesus Christ is God, and the demons know it. Also, I noticed that the demons did not care if I used Mary's name. At one point, I had also tried using holy water to ward off the

---

[12] This took place back in 2006. Both of my grandmothers passed away in early 2017. This proves that the entities were wanting to scare me with lies.

demons, which didn't work. Life is not always like a Hollywood movie, especially when it comes to exorcisms or deliverance from supernatural evil. *Things* don't work. *Things* won't deliver, protect, or heal you from evil in the spiritual realm.

The voice to my left ear would pray with me, especially when I would forget a prayer. I could feel his breath on my face. I could also hear John's voice praying with me. I could hear angels singing in the background. It was insane. Looking back, this was an illusion to make me believe that John's voice was a good spirit and that angels were with me. At some point, I had also heard, "You don't know who you are messing with!" "You are supposed to be my bride." "You married me." "I can offer you fame and fortune if you will be my bride in Hell," which I declined. This was claimed to be said by Satan. It is interesting to note that Dina's voice had also told me a few times that I didn't know who I was messing with.

I then had a strange sensation of power come over me. It was a good power. I stood up and started telling the demons that they had a life in Hell to look forward to, and they should turn their demon lives around to Jesus Christ. I told them that Jesus Christ was love, and they would never experience love or peace without Jesus Christ. Some of the demons claimed it might be a good idea, others said Satan wouldn't have it, but in any event, no one appeared to leave. Then, I heard a voice claiming to be Lucifer. He said that he was going to give me his power so that I could see if I liked it or not. I told him that I didn't want his power, but I felt a strong evil power build up inside me that I did not like. I had a foul taste in my mouth. I told him repeatedly that I did not want his power or anything to do with him. Lucifer told me that I had over twenty demons inside of me. I don't know if I had that many or not, but I now know Lucifer is the Father of Lies. Jesus said:

> "You are of your father the devil, and your will is to do your father's desires. He was a murderer from the beginning and does not stand in the truth, because there is no truth in him. When he lies, he speaks out of his own character, for he is a liar and the father of lies." John 8:44 ESV

I heard so many voices that I couldn't keep up. I knew that I wasn't going to get any sleep if I stayed home, so I got in my car around 11:00 p.m. and headed for the nearest Roman Catholic Church. I had an idea to sit in the chapel. This wasn't the first time. As soon as I walked into the Chapel, everything went silent immediately. However, I began to slightly make out the voice of three demons telling each other that they were leaving. I sat there dozing on and off, trying to sleep, but then I started hearing John asking me if I would marry him. One time I heard that "John's demon" would never leave me alone. Other times I would hear that I was chosen by God.

The next night, I went to the "Lourdes Grotto and Guadalupe Tepeyac," which is referred to by the "Oblate Missions Missionary Association of Mary Immaculate," on their website as the "Spiritual Center of the Missionary Association Mary Immaculate and Oblate Missions." People in San Antonio call it "The Grotto." I walked around and sat down next to a statue of Jesus Christ. I prayed that He would save me. I heard a voice tell me that I was chosen by Jesus Christ to write a book. This surprised me. The voice would not tell me why I was chosen to write a book or what the book was supposed to be about. I was told that Larry is really an angel, but that the demon is making me think that Larry is a demon. The demon twists Larry's words around just like he did mine. I had been keeping journals, so I decided to continue writing about what was happening to me.

Later, I was told by the voices that if I attended mass and stopped smoking cigarettes that I would not hear them anymore. I didn't stop smoking, but I went to another mass. It was strange because I could not focus on the mass. I kept hearing two comedians' voices overpowering the priest's words. These voices appeared funny and friendly, but I've realized that "funny" and "appearing friendly" doesn't always mean "friend." *If the voices had wanted me to attend mass, why didn't they allow me to concentrate?*

Later, Larry, John, and Dina were all present again and we all heard more "information" about each other. The night ended with me having a long conversation with John. I told him to stay with his wife and children, and what we did was wrong. I then prayed for John and Dina. I prayed that they would work their problems out and stay together. It appeared that it was angels who intervened that night and told others to let me sleep. I got to sleep again.

Another night, my parents were coming into town to bring my son back to me so that I could take him back to his dad's house. I told them that I would wait for them at a grocery store parking lot. I never told them what was going on. By the time they got there, I had my car seat all the way back and felt like my body was cooking. I felt more pain than ever. I had heard aliens telling me that they were about to kill me, but before that, other aliens had been claiming they would fight "demon butt." It was all so strange. I could smell my body cooking. There was no way that I could get up out of the car to walk on my own. I felt like I was in a trance. It was a good that my son wasn't living with me. My parents pulled up and were horrified to find me in that condition. They got me out of my car and put me in the back seat of their truck, and we all took my son home. I left my car in the grocery store parking lot.

I told my parents that I was told by the voices to stay away from my house, and to live somewhere else. My parents checked us into a hotel room. I went outside to smoke a cigarette and prayed again for John and Dina's marriage. I could hear Dina thanking me for praying for them. I went back into the hotel room, but because I could still hear other voices, I asked my mom and dad to please pray the rosary with me. We did, and my parents fell asleep. While they were sleeping, my mouth opened, and I began praying what seemed to be the rosary at a high-rate of speed. My mouth began moving so fast that I could not understand the prayers. It was like someone else was using my mouth. I found a Bible in the hotel room and slept with it under my pillow. I was so happy that my parents were there with me though!

The next morning, I told my parents that I did not want to live in that house anymore. I thought it was haunted. I wanted to move. They decided to allow some friends of mine to move in and rent it from them. I called my friend Shelly. She said that I could live with her as long as I needed. My parents and I went to my house to start packing and moving. I could hardly function

As soon as I walked into my bedroom, approximately twenty or more voices started talking to me. It was overwhelming. One was telling me to hurt myself with some scissors, but I knew better. I wondered about people who would harm themselves or others because they heard voices, as if they didn't know it was wrong, or that it would cause harm. I was thankful I hadn't reached that point. I couldn't take the noise, so I went outside and stood in the front yard and prayed while I threw up what I had believed to be demons. The taste was dreadful, but I had thought that God was removing the demons from my body. This was a trick. No demon was leaving, and if he or she was, he or she was coming right back in, so it seemed. My dad walked outside and saw me doing this. He looked worried. We all went back to the hotel room for the night.

Soon after, my parents spoke to my boss about getting me into a hospital. My boss agreed. My parents received some information from one of my neighbors on how to get me admitted quickly. Once we were at the hospital, I was quickly directed to the psychiatric floor for evaluation. They told me that they wanted to keep me there a few days, and if I chose to stay, I could not leave the hospital until the doctors approved. I was very concerned about my job. My boss was like a second dad to me, and I knew he needed me, but after talking to my parents, I agreed. The voices told me that they would be leaving while I was in the hospital. They said something about how they would be detected if the medicine didn't appear to work. Everything went quiet for a while. I was in the hospital for two weeks. I was very worried about my boss and job. I finally got to a point where I would socialize with the other patients only because I was told that I had to in order to be released. They put me in a room with several doctors and/or students who all sat around and listened to me tell them what was happening. Their faces looked as though they had never heard anything so crazy in their lives. I was hoping that what I was sharing wasn't the most insane thing they have ever heard. I was hoping that I wasn't worse off than everyone else they had diagnosed. I was put on several drugs.

I was eating well again; three meals a day. The food was very good. I even put on some weight. After released, my parents drove me to Shelly's house where I was to live. Nicole stayed there, too, at times. My parents had done all the moving for me while I was hospitalized. Also, my boss was happy to see me. I took my medication for a few weeks, but it made me feel rigid and weird, and it was impossible for me to comfortably work. Since I was only hearing, "I love you so much" and still feeling sensations, I figured it was safe for me to stop taking the medicine. This was in January of 2007.

Aside from hearing "I love you so much," and still feeling sensations, not much else happened other than me hitting an intense depression falsely believing that Jesus Christ didn't want to save me. I had pulled away from faith in Him. I felt like God had forsaken me because He didn't answer my prayers the way I wanted. I knew that turning my back from God was making me more depressed. I also knew that Hell is absent of God; absent of spiritual life. Every day I wished to be dead the moment I opened my eyes. It took every ounce of strength I had to get up out of bed and walk to the bathroom to brush my teeth or take a shower. Simple tasks required all my willpower and strength. I felt as though I were moving in thick mud that was fighting against me living. I was ridden with severe anxiety and uncomfortable in my own skin for hours at times. There was no peace. I had no social life. I didn't want to talk to anyone. All I wanted to do was to lie in my room and sleep, so I could avoid the misery of being awake.

Things were going well for Shelly. She met a nice man and they started going to church on Sundays. They invited me. I went a few times, but I didn't understand why Christians held up their hands in church. They looked so happy and peaceful; they had energy. I went down to pray at the altar when the pastor asked, but nothing seemed to change then. The people seemed very different than me.

Chapter Eleven
A Miracle...Please...

I WANTED TO have my own place, so I got an apartment in July of 2007. Nicole stayed with me for a short time. That December of 2007, almost a year after being released from the hospital, I met a guy on a dating site named Roy. I was still very depressed and wasn't quite sure if I was ready for dating, but still tried. He broke up with me after a few weeks. We got back together, and I broke up with him. We got back together, and he broke up with me again. A few days later, February 8, 2008, I woke up and my depression was completely gone. It was just gone. This was strange because I should have been sad about the breakup, but it felt like a dark cloud had finally been lifted off me.

Also, I had remembered that Roy was not for Jesus Christ. To 'fit in' with him, I initially denied Christ, which was wrong. I later told Roy that I still believed in Jesus. Oddly, we got back together, for a short while, and he asked me to marry him. He was making plans for our future and showed me a photograph of ring he had ordered for me. I honestly did not want to marry him because it didn't feel right, but after a fit of jealousy, he broke up with me again in June of 2008, because he thought I had cheated on him with one of my guy friends, Brad. At that time, the voices came right back but so did my total faith in God! I felt as though my soul was up for grabs!

Once it was over between us, I began going out for more drinks and conversation with Brad. Things quickly turned into an intimate relationship with Brad, but we weren't a couple. Brad had introduced me to some magician friends of his, and we would hang out with them at a magic bar. I had become close friends with one of them named Pete who ended up in a serious relationship with one of my close girlfriends, Katheryn. We would spend nights going from parties to bars watching magic tricks, but some of the dark and heavy close-up magic, which included mind reading, made me feel sick. Pete and a close magician friend of his said that my face looked white one night, so they both decided to stop. They said that other people had the same type of reaction to that type of magic. I had felt that the force of magic that night was evil. I felt a disgust for it.

Later, because I was seeking something to make me feel better, I snorted a street drug I had never done. I later met Brad and some other friends at a bar to watch a local band. I told Brad that I was high. A few hours into watching a band, we all decided to leave. Brad walked me to my car, looked me in the eyes and said, "I don't like you like that. I'll talk to you later." I said, "Okay," and got in my car and drove home.

At first, I was angry and hurt, but I quickly understood that he was right. He made me realize that I had a problem, and my behavior was a contributing factor, if not the entire factor. It wasn't only about hearing voices. It was everything. I realized that I wouldn't be good enough for anyone; not even myself. I realized how I had been blaming others for my problems without taking much accountability for my part, except for understanding some of "my part" in my failed marriage to Wes. It was strange because I also had a lot of self-hatred inside, and I beat myself up emotionally. One night while spending the night at Brad's house, I heard a voice say something about sin and death and about me having to pay a penalty. I believed that voice, and I was terrified of going to Hell, so I soon stopped having sex with Brad. We remained friends though.

Physically, I was sick. My diet was horrible. My health was waning. I was a size 0 at Old Navy. I lived on large fountain drinks, powered donuts, Whataburger meals, sodas, large bags of Ruffles chips, smoked cigarettes, dabbled in occasional recreational drug use, and took too much Adderall. Family and friends were telling me to check back into the hospital, but I wasn't so sure.

Instead, I begged in tearful desperation for God to tell me what He wanted me to do. I heard a new voice tell me to buy a King James Bible, and look for a book called Deliverance online. I don't know why the King James version was the choice, but I may have bought a 'bad translation,' if not told. Plus, I had heard of the King James Bible before, so I understood clearly. The voice explained that the book Deliverance would have an index to help me find the information that I needed. I was also told to look up the definitions of the words *deliverance, salvation,* and *sanctification.* I was told to stop sinning in specific areas. I was so happy to get all this information. I went to work and began an internet search for the word "deliverance" and found a PDF of a book online now titled, *Major Christian Deliverance Principles: Keys for Self-Deliverance and Ministry* by Eric Gondwe. This book had a huge impact on me.[13]

The book is about spiritual warfare. It had an index. I downloaded and printed it out while at work. I began reading it right away. I also bought a King James Bible and looked up the definitions of the words *deliverance, salvation,* and *sanctification.* I also sent Mr. Gondwe an email explaining what I was experiencing. He then sent me Chapter 13 from another book of his located online titled *Breaking Spiritual Strongholds and Healing the Wounded Spirit: Dealing with*

---

[13] http://www.deliveranceministrybooks.com/html/christian-deliverance-book.html

Root Causes.[14] Gondwe's books pointed me to Jesus Christ, His power, and His Word. You can also find a book today titled *Overcoming demonic oppression, Schizophrenia & Psychosis: Christian Guide Book*.[15]

The specific chapter Gondwe sent explained that I had been involved in occult practices, which described nearly every symptom I had of tapping into the spiritual realm. It pointed me to scripture and explained strongholds and how the enemy can gain a stronghold. His books also told me to focus on Jesus Christ. I read scripture in his books and began reading the New Testament. In reading the New Testament, I came across the following:

> Then Jesus told his disciples, "If anyone would come after me, let him deny himself and take up his cross and follow me. For whoever would save his life will lose it, but whoever loses his life for my sake will find it." Matthew 16:24-25 ESV

As I read, I understood. I knew Jesus Christ wanted me to follow Him, and I could not follow Him if I did not know Him. I could not know Him if I did not read His Word. I was beginning to understand that God wanted me to seek

---

[14] http://www.spiritualwarfaredeliverance.com/books/o8-breaking-spiritual-strongholds-healing-wounded-spirit/index.html
[15] http://www.deliveranceministrybooks.com/html/overcoming-demonic-oppression-book.html

Him and know Him. He wanted a relationship with me.

Shortly after this time period, Roy came over to see me, and unfortunately, we were physically intimate, even though I had no interest in getting back together with him. I'm not sure if he had an interest either. I don't remember. I remember telling Roy about what I had learned about Jesus Christ. I was starting to understand Jesus, but I hadn't fully submitted to His Lordship yet.

I continued to read my Bible and pray. I also continued to read Gondwe's books. During this time, my psychiatrist suggested that I take a new medicine to reduce the voices. I took the new medication one night. I could still hear voices, but they were faint. However, the dose made me sleepy and knocked me out.

After that night, I believed God wanted me to work on the root of the problems. If I just covered up the symptoms, the problem or problems would still be there. If I didn't see that a problem existed, I wouldn't be able to work on it. Plus, I was not a danger to myself or others, so I decided to discontinue taking anymore medication, other than Adderall. I do not recommend anyone doing this without first praying about it and speaking to his or her doctor.

God wanted my mind focused on Him and His Word. I wouldn't be able to do that on strong medication that made my brain foggy and susceptible to hearing and absorbing lies. There was a significant battle going on for my mind, and I had a hard time controlling my own thoughts on the medication.

I told my psychiatrist that I didn't want any more medication and that it was a spiritual issue. She respected my decision. I kept reading the Bible and praying for God to help me. I kept asking God if He would close the spiritual realm, but nothing changed right away. I finally realized that perhaps I needed to accept what I was hearing and that it may be a part of His plan for me. I finally told God that I would listen to the voices and accept the fact that He wants me to hear them.

I had been learning discernment through hearing the voices. I was learning so much from reading God's Word, hearing voices of light, and then hearing the enemy's voice. It was tough because I had learned that the enemy's voice can sound like a voice of light.

"And no marvel; for even Satan fashioneth himself into an angel of light." 2 Corinthians 11:14 KJV

A lot of who I thought was God was Satan, especially that condemning voice, and that voice that told me that I could have fame and wealth, if I would just worship him. I realized that God wasn't having me seek fame, wealth, and stuff. He knew those things were not what I needed. Look at all the people who have fame and wealth who are miserable. I learned that God is Holy, and He is a being who created me, loves me, and was calling me to repent. He is also just and merciful. He wanted me to know Him, which seemed unbelievable. I couldn't believe I had been treating Him like a 'genie in a bottle.' He is not our slave or our servant. We are not his god, and we are not to boss Him around and make demands on Him.

I learned that Jesus Christ was not the voice yelling at me for not being in proper position while I prayed. For example, I would get on my knees, and hear, "stand up!" I would stand up and hear, "get on your knees!" This would happen a few times, as if I just couldn't get it right, as if God was frustrated and impatient. I later learned that the enemy wanted me to believe that God was intolerant and upset with me, all while I was trying to find my way to Christ.

In reading His Word, I noted how Jesus Christ asks us to follow Him. People approached Him to be delivered and healed. He didn't scream at them. Jesus delivered and healed them and asked them to repent and "sin no more." He didn't yell.

Satan, "the voices," or even "thoughts I had" seemed to want me to feel as though God hated me and that He was difficult to please, so I would not want to read His Word or follow Him. The Bible shows that Jesus didn't push people away as they were seeking Him. Satan wanted me to believe lies about God in order to keep me away from Jesus Christ. I realized later that Satan had wanted me to believe that 'God was with me,' when He wasn't. I wrote a journal entry on September 17, 2008:

> Today I heard, Be strong and hold fast because Jesus Christ is about to deliver you. Told to read Psalm 24 [and] 25 Told to Read Breaking Strongholds – and to <u>look up salvation and ask Jesus Christ for salvation</u> – study the Psalm that you were told to read tonight and practice everything. Keep God in your mind, heart, spirit, and soul, worship and pray. [Emphasis Added]

I heard another voice, too, and wrote about it. The spirit that I heard told me he was the anti-[C]hrist and that he was coming soon. I was repeatedly being asked to just answer one question, and it was about John. I ignored the demon and did not respond. Psalm 25 states:

> Unto thee, O Jehovah, do I lift up my soul. O my God, in thee have I trusted, Let me not be put to shame; Let not mine enemies triumph over me. Yea, none that wait for thee shall be put to shame: They shall be put to shame that deal treacherously without cause. Show me thy ways, O Jehovah; Teach me thy paths. Guide me in thy truth, and teach me; For thou art the God of my salvation; For thee do I wait all the day. Remember, O Jehovah, thy tender mercies and

thy lovingkindness; For they have been ever of old. Remember not the sins of my youth, nor my transgressions: According to thy lovingkindness remember thou me, For thy goodness' sake, O Jehovah. Good and upright is Jehovah: Therefore will he instruct sinners in the way. The meek will he guide in justice; And the meek will he teach his way. All the paths of Jehovah are lovingkindness and truth Unto such as keep his covenant and his testimonies. For thy name's sake, O Jehovah, Pardon mine iniquity, for it is great. What man is he that feareth Jehovah? Him shall he instruct in the way that he shall choose. His soul shall dwell at ease; And his seed shall inherit the land. The friendship of Jehovah is with them that fear him; And he will show them his covenant. Mine eyes are ever toward Jehovah; For he will pluck my feet out of the net. Turn thee unto me, and have mercy upon me; For I am desolate and afflicted. The troubles of my heart are enlarged: Oh bring thou me out of my distresses. Consider mine affliction and my travail; And forgive all my sins. Consider mine enemies, for they are many; And they hate me with cruel hatred. Oh keep my soul, and deliver me: Let me not be put to shame, for I take refuge in thee. Let integrity and uprightness preserve me, For I wait for thee. Redeem Israel, O God, Out all of his troubles. Psalms 25:1-22 ASV

Chapter Twelve
Jesus Christ Changes Lives

THE DEMONIC VOICES had begun to fade. I started to hear love and encouragement most of the time. After reading the Bible, I had still gone out with friends to clubs, but my perception was beginning to change. Unfortunately, the day I made the September 17, 2008, journal entry, I was coming down off the same street drug I had taken recently. That night I experienced unbearable mental and spiritual agony. I was hurting bad. I clearly knew God was asking me if I wanted to follow Him. I didn't hear this as an audible voice. I just knew that Jesus Christ was asking me that question. This was the first time in my life that I felt like I had to make a choice right then. I understood. I could keep on following myself, or I could lose my life for Jesus, and follow Him.

I was afraid to say "yes" because I was afraid of the unknown and didn't know what God had planned for me. I knew in my heart that if I chose Him, I was telling Him to do whatever He wanted with me. I then asked God what He would do with me if I said "yes." I told Him that I didn't want to be like Mother Teresa, but I knew that my life couldn't get

89

any worse. The Holy Spirit impressed upon me – "You've been your own little god all your life. How's that working out?" That caught my attention because it wasn't working out. I was a horrible little god! I knew He was telling me that whatever He had to offer would be much better. I knew that I was not going to make it without Him. I agreed that my lordship over my life wasn't working out, and I cried out answering, "Please take over my whole life!"

I knew at that moment that I had completely given myself to Him and trusted Him to do whatever He wanted to do with me. I turned away from self (my "lordship"), and my need to control my own life (repented) and instead decided to submit entirely to His Lordship over every area of my life. I didn't bother with the thought of **how** I was going to do His will. I must have known in my heart that He was going to help me.

I then laid in bed crying with the lights out. It wasn't long before I heard two of the most beautiful voices. Two or more male voices were speaking gently and in a loving manner telling me that the Adderall is hurting my brain, and I don't need to take it anymore. I could sense deep love. I couldn't believe I wasn't being condemned. The male voices were not angry with me. I knew God didn't want me to harm myself. I heard the voices talking among themselves. I remember they were healing me and talked about my brain and how I would be "good as new." I finally fell asleep.

When I woke up the next morning, I walked over to my purse to get my Adderall, like every morning, but I had no desire to take it. I was holding it in my hand seeing the contents of the bottle as if it were a piece of worthless trash. I felt very awake. I felt good, which was strange. I threw away the full bottle.

Later, while at work, I could hear the Holy Spirit filling my mind with truths letting me know that I was not worthless and that I am loved. I was crying soft tears of joy with the good news that I wasn't worthless. It felt like rubber bands of bondage were breaking apart and a flood of love, self-worth, and completeness filled me up. I felt whole for the first time. I felt free! I could feel the Holy Spirit inside of me! The Holy Spirit led me to confess many sins later when I got home. He gave me godly sorrow for my sins. Not condemnation but a genuine sorrow for the first time for sinning against God. After I confessed, I knew that God wanted me to forgive myself. His forgiveness is enough. His suffering for my sins and dying on the cross was sufficient.[16] The Greek New

---

[16] Much later I learned that the Latin Vulgate was translated from the Greek New Testament manuscripts. As noted in The KJV New Testament Greek Lexicon, the Greek manuscripts use the words metanoeō (G3340), and metanoia (G3341), which both mean repent or repentance.
https://www.biblestudytools.com/lexicons/greek/kjv/metanoeo.html
However, the Latin Vulgate uses a word that describes penance. When I was Catholic, I had been taught to recite prayers as a form of punishment to atone for my sins. On the cross, Jesus Christ said, "*It is*

Testament Manuscripts[17] say nothing of penance, but instead use words that define repentance. It speaks of love and joy for those who have the Holy Spirit. Also, those who have the Holy Spirit are considered Saints and Priests in God's eyes. "The Church" is the Spiritual "Body of Christ," which means all those who have received the Holy Spirit. We are to repent of our sins even as we follow Christ. The Holy Spirit enables us to do so. *"Bear fruit in keeping with repentance."* Matthew 3:8 ESV.

Also, Christ said, *"Ye shall know them by their fruits."* Matthew 7:16 KJV. He also says to abide in Him and bear fruit, *"I am the vine, ye are the branches: He that abideth in me, and I in him, the same bringeth forth much fruit: for without me ye can do nothing."* John 15:5 KJV.

---

finished," and he bowed his head and gave up his spirit." John 19:30 ESV.

Also, the Catholic Public Domain Version (CPDV) in Acts 17:30 states, *"And indeed, God, having looked down to see the ignorance of these times, has now announced to men that everyone everywhere should do penance."* However, according to the KJV w/Strong's Numbers, the Greek New Testament in Acts 17:30 uses the word metanoeō (G3340), not penance, which changes the meaning. Acts 17:30 ESV states, *"The times of ignorance God overlooked, but now he commands all people everywhere to repent."* https://www.biblestudytools.com/esv/acts/17-30.html

[17] http://www.csntm.org/Manuscript and https://www.biblestudytools.com/interlinear-bible/

The voices went away, and so did the depression, mood swings, and anxiety.[18] I told my psychiatrist that I wouldn't be taking anymore Adderall, or any other medication, and that I was healed. She was trying to figure out if my taking that one medication had triggered something that helped me "snap" out of everything, but later she told me that she did believe that something spiritual was going on. She agreed that I didn't need any more medication.

---

[18] The voices were not from the John I had known, or his former wife. John has read a draft of this book. We have spoken a few times about what happened. He has apologized, and I forgive him. I have also communicated with his now former wife. She did not know about me during that time, so no one was telepathically communicating with me. Demons throw out half-truths to try and distract people from sanity and from finding or following Jesus Christ.

The Bible says that every spirit needs to be tested to see if his or her actions, words, and motives line up with the Word of God. Scripture says, *"Beloved, believe not every spirit, but try the spirits whether they are of God: because many false prophets are gone out into the world."* 1 John 4:1 KJV. Scripture also says, *"And no marvel; for Satan himself is transformed into an angel of light. Therefore it is no great thing if his ministers also be transformed as the ministers of righteousness; whose end shall be according to their works."* 2 Corinthians 11:14-15 KJV.

Also, there are demonic tongues and demonic transference can take place through the laying on of hands in some churches, so we should be careful to not allow anyone to lay their hands on us or pray over us in a tongue that we do not understand. Also, any deception, illusion, or lie is not of the truth, and therefore is not of God. There is no deceit in God. 1 John 2:21 ESV and Revelation 22:15 ESV

God also said, *"My people are destroyed for lack of knowledge..."* Hosea 4:6 ESV. Jesus Christ said, *"And you will know the truth, and the truth will set you free."* John 8:32 ESV

I woke up early on a Saturday ready to start the day, which was a miracle. I couldn't believe I was up before 11:00 a.m. I felt so alive and energized, not a nervous and spastic energy, but a *full, peaceful, vibrant, joyful energy.* We hear of fairy tales with happy endings all the time, but this is better than any fairy tale I had ever heard, and it is true! I didn't know God was going to make me feel good inside!

I learned that life is not about "survival of the fittest," as I was as weak as a person could get when I gave my life to Christ. I was coming down off a street drug, had schizoaffective disorder, Attention Deficit Disorder, depression, anxiety, a prescription drug addiction, and a cigarette addiction. I was a size 0 and fading away. My mother thought I was anorexic. People thought I was going to die. I woke up delivered and stronger than ever because of God changing me and living inside of me!

The Lord taught me that life is not about visualizing who I want to be, and then pretending to be that person, or expecting to receive what I request from the "universe," which is a created *thing.* The good life is in surrender and knowing Jesus Christ as our Lord and Savior. We are all born into sin, but once we are reconciled to Him, we are remade, born again. It is then when we find out who we are because we have been restored with our Maker. He then equips each of us to carry out His mission for our lives. *Nothing* comes close to knowing Him. He is my treasure!

I began craving fruit and started cleaning my apartment. I kept changing. I didn't know where to go to church, so I went to a Catholic mass and a woman giving announcements had mentioned that the Catholic teachings were equal to that of the Bible. From reading the Bible, I found out that many of the Roman Catholic Church's teachings were different than the biblical teachings of Jesus Christ and His first apostles, which includes Apostle Peter. The doctrine set out in the Letters of Peter in the New Testament are a source of truth, but it differs from the Catholic Church on some vital issues. I was surprised to find the truth to be better! I had to repent of self-rule, but I didn't have to 'be good first' or try to earn grace. I'm not supposed to walk around feeling guilty after receiving the Holy Spirit because it is Him who frees me from being a slave to sin and who gives me joy! I'm supposed to have joy and peace. The word gospel means "good news."

Also, in examining Jesus Christ's character, we still need to look at the Old Testament to understand God (since Christ is God and is One with the Father), but those who trust and follow Jesus Christ are now under the New Covenant. Many churches are filled with false teachings (errors) these days, so it can be difficult to find a bible-based church that holds to proper doctrine.

I decided that I would trust Jesus Christ over anyone, since He is God. I had been following false doctrine, and my own selfish desires instead of seeking and following Jesus

Christ. If I am indeed a Christian, then no one's words would trump that of Jesus Christ! He is Boss over all! If I don't think He's boss over all, then how can I call myself a Christian? A Christian is a Christ-follower, but I had labeled myself a Christian in the past when I did not know Christ. I did not have the Holy Spirit dwelling in me. I was not saved. I did not change before. I did not have the fruits of the Holy Spirit before. I did not experience any change as a child when I was water baptized or when I received confirmation. Instead, I repented at the age of 38 after hearing the gospel of truth, like Ephesians 1:13 KJV states, *"In whom ye also trusted, after that ye heard the word of truth, the gospel of your salvation: in whom also after that ye believed, ye were sealed with that holy Spirit of promise."*

However, I went to another mass, but I couldn't stop crying, so I had to leave. I had been scared that God was going to be mad at me for leaving mass, but He wasn't mad. I began praying for God to show me where to go to church. I heard a thought run through my mind, "Remember that church you've driven by for years and have always felt an urge to attend? Go to that church." I had remembered in reading Gondwe's deliverance book to look for a church whose leaders and members showed the fruits of The Holy Spirit.

"But the fruit of the Spirit is love, joy, peace, patience, kindness, goodness, faithfulness, gentleness, self-control; against such things, there is no law." Galatians 5:22-23 ESV

The next Sunday, I walked through the doors of that church. I could see the fruits of the Holy Spirit in the people holding the doors open. Smiling people full of joy!

A member, and now friend, asked if I wanted to do a four-week study on Christ. She took me through a One on One Discipleship folder and explained what I needed to know about my relationship with Jesus Christ vs. my fellowship with Him. It was critical that I understood that the Christian Bible is the source of truth by which we are to measure proper doctrine.

"Every scripture inspired of God is also profitable for teaching, for reproof, for correction, for instruction which is in righteousness." 2 Timothy 3:16 ASV

I was learning that I needed to saturate myself in the truth so that I could discern false doctrine and know the Lord's will. I began to see that He made my will line up with His. I started working out and having ideas for ministry. I was on fire for God, and I still am! I cannot get over His love!

It's been over ten years since the night that I gave my life to Christ. I still feel like I am in a fairy tale, much of the time. Sure, I have rough days, and rough seasons, but now the "GOD of the universe," the Father, Son, and the Holy Spirit, protects me, provides for me, and sustains me *through everything*. He holds me above breaking points. He's my Lord, my best friend, and is all worthy!

I found that knowing Christ, and submitting to Him in obedience, is the good life. Also, He empowers us to follow Him.

> "A new heart also will I give you, and a new spirit will I put within you: and I will take away the stony heart out of your flesh, and I will give you an heart of flesh." Ezekiel 36-26 KJV

> "Therefore if anyone is in Christ, he is a new creation. The old has passed away. Behold, the new has come!" 2 Corinthians 5:17 KJV

With my background of being exposed to Satanism, new age practices, "positive thinking myself into lies," and doing drugs, there was always something missing. Even when I had my family around, cash on hand, romantic love, and tons of friends, I was still missing God. It was Him who I was searching for the entire time. We all are or were. We look for Him because we were made to be in a relationship with Him. We cannot function like we were originally intended to function because we are born into sin, broken from a relationship with Him, which is why we must be born-again (receive the Holy Spirit) and restored to have spiritual life.

However, sometimes we think we only need that person, this or that job, or enough money to pay the rent, buy a car, and pay bills, and yes, we do have basic needs and wants, but placing God first is the most critical need. Once we do that, He satisfies every single need and quenches every thirst!

> "But seek ye first his kingdom, and his righteousness; and all these things shall be added unto you." Matthew 6:33 ASV

My perception, emotions, and behavior have changed. I also have more self-control and am pulsating with life and energy! The Lord had to humble me so that I could see my need for him. He regenerated me and began helping me to see, to spiritually perceive, and to hear, to spiritually listen to Him.

Jesus Christ uses the word "repent" over and over in the Bible, which is why I was originally going to title this book *Remade From Rue*. One definition of Rue means repentance. Of course, the repentance itself didn't save me, but it was necessary. Jesus Christ is the One who saved me. He changed my heart and helped me see that I needed to repent. He also helped me to repent. I was remade by Christ. Christ was key. He calls sinners to repent so that they can live the good life with Him!

"The Lord is not slow to fulfill his promise as some count slowness, but is patient toward you, not wishing that nay should perish, but that all should reach repentance." 2 Peter 3:9 ESV

If you want to know Jesus Christ, the first steps I'd suggest are the following:

1.   Pray to the Father for your salvation, to receive His Holy Spirit, and for help reading the Bible. Pray in Jesus Christ's name.

2.   Begin reading one of the first four books (gospels) in the New Testament (Mark, Matthew, Luke, or John). If you don't have a Bible, you can use free online or mobile Bible software;[19]

3.   If you have any questions regarding which Bible translation to use, ASV, ESV, and the KJV are good. If you want to know a little more about translations, you can read this article[20];

4.   Read Eric Gondwe's online book *Christian Deliverance*;[21]

5.   Read Eric Gondwe's online book *Breaking Spiritual Strongholds*[22] (if you're hearing voices or

---

[19] http://www.e-sword.net or http://www.bible.com
[20] http://www.princessofthemosthighking.com/which-bible-translation-should-you-use/
[21] http://www.deliveranceministrybooks.com/html/christian-deliverance-book.htm
[22] http://www.spiritualwarfaredeliverance.com/books/08-breaking-spiritual-strongholds-healing-wounded-spirit/index.html

experiencing demonic activity, Chapter 13 will be extremely informative);

6.   Find a church that holds the Bible as authoritative; and,

7.   Please know that you can look up answers to any questions that you may have at http://www.gotquestions.org

If you're hearing voices: Keep your mind focused on Jesus Christ, His Word, His promises, and His power. Try not to focus on anything they're saying. They want to "reel you in" to keep you distracted. They will throw out half-truths 'here and there' to get you interested in listening. In addition to the above, focus on Christ and His power! I have all the above links posted on two of my websites.[23]

Some don't believe me, but a person can't "positive" away several mental illnesses, break several additions, change her character, perform better at work, make better grades, and then fill herself up with a great deal of energy, joy, and love. How could a "positive" mentality surface while illness and addictions are broken while coming down off a street drug right after asking Jesus Christ to take over my life? How could deliverance of those illnesses and issues have lasted over ten years, if it were not true? I have not taken any

---

[23] http://www.evematheny.com/ and
http://princessofthemosthighking.com/

medication for any mental illness since that night in September 2008. Because of Jesus Christ, I went from a spiritually dead girl to being remade; a new creation in Christ. *"Therefore, if anyone is in Christ, he is a new creation. The old has passed away; behold, the new has come."* 2 Corinthians 5:17 ESV

Millions of people have stories like mine. You probably won't hear these stories on the news stations, but some are shared in books, on the web, and in Christian Churches.

Please know that some people have given their lives to follow Christ but have later been led astray by false doctrine and/or sin, so since I am still learning who is part of what church and what movement, I cannot recommend many people to disciple, but I will add a list of resources on my author website.

I have been surprised at the number of labeled "Christian" evangelists who are teaching false doctrine, knowingly or unknowingly, so please do not blindly trust just any pastor or church. If a pastor refuses to talk about sin, repenting from sin, Hell, or rejects Jesus Christ as being God, or rejects Jesus Christ as being the only way the Father, or exalts born-again Christians or man as being equal to Jesus Christ, then those are false teachers or Christians who are in bondage to lies.

That said, you can find testimonies from the former vocalist of rock band Flyleaf, Lacey Sturm and two former members of the rock band Korn. Annie Liberty, a high-class former prostitute, shares her story along with other former prostitutes on YouTube. I Am Second[24] shares celebrity testimonies. Former atheists or agnostics like Lee Strobel and Josh McDowell, who both sought out to discredit Jesus Christ, both found Him. For more information, you can read Lee Strobel's book *The Case for Christ*, and Josh McDowell and Sean McDowell's book *More Than a Carpenter* (one of my favorite books).

Also, former devil worshiper John Ramirez explains how he came to Jesus Christ in various YouTube videos and in his book *Out of the Devil's Cauldron*.

However, there are tons of Christian testimonies on YouTube, and the common denominator is Jesus Christ!

---

[24] http://www.iamsecond.com

I love Jesus Christ! I am a Christ-follower before anything or anyone. I also love the season of Spring. The beach. Flowers. Law. Painting. Writing. I also love spending time with my family and friends!

I'm purposely single meaning that I choose not to date. I LOVE being single because I can spend more alone time with God! I figure that if God wants me to get married again (this time as a born-again Christian), He will let me know and make it happen, but as of right now, I don't have an interest.

As far as my occupation, I recently resigned from working as a full-time Lead Paralegal for a law firm in Houston. I was about to be promoted to a Paralegal Manger, but I knew that God was calling me to leave. I have been in the legal field for over twenty years, and I love working as a paralegal. However, most of my former jobs have required a lot of overtime, which has made it difficult to focus on completing school. I also have two side ministries, which are a priority, as well. Therefore, I am working on finding a source of income that will allow me to pay my bills while completing college and managing side ministries!

God willing, I will be attending college this year to complete a Bachelor of Applied Science Degree in Management at Wayland Baptist University. I have ten more classes. n Ministry or Divinity Degree. However, law school has also been on my mind. As a result, I am going to focus on the priorities and keep praying about the direction God wants me to take. I hold a Paralegal Certificate, and I am a Certified Belief Therapist with The Therapon Institute, which is a religious organization.[25]

Also, I am in a leadership program with a women's organization called Inspire Women.[26] I have grown so much from being in this program!

As far as my religious beliefs, they line up with the Baptist Statement of Faith[27]. I attend a Southern Baptist Church in Texas.

I have two ministries that I manage. I have one where I share my testimony through various means (this book, my author website, and my YouTube Channel[28]) and another with the ultimate goal to grow it into a productive Christen women's blog, vlog, podcast, and magazine that will have other Christ-followers sharing blogs and articles.[29]

The ministry initially started in 2014 when I founded it as a non-profit organization called Princess of the Most High King. We published one digital magazine. However, we

---

[25] https://therapon.org/
[26] https://inspirewomen.org/
[27] http://www.sbc.net/bfm2000/bfm2000.asp
[28] http://www.evematheny.com/ and
https://www.youtube.com/c/evematheny
[29] http://www.princessofthemosthighking.com/ and
https://www.youtube.com/channel/UC4JRXhS15VvNVpoUk30KQGg?

dissolved. Therefore, in 2017, I formed Princess of the Most High King as an LLC, but with the same mission to spread the good news, disciple, and build-up women in the church! It is still a baby ministry, but my future goals include having one or two people help manage the ministry.

As far as other ministries, I have served as a Whole Hearts Representative and a Grace Representative at Grace Point Church in San Antonio. I have also helped lead a boundaries class and served the homeless with a church group. In addition, I have shared my testimony with various groups of people in the church, outside the church, and online through my websites and YouTube Channels.

I began writing songs (lyrics and melodies) after giving my life to Christ. You will see some of those songs posted on my author website and YouTube Channel. Since I am not developed in this area, I would love to take voice lessons, guitar lessons, and spend more time developing the skill of writing music! Thank you again for reading!

Truths Learned

God is real. His design is everywhere. In the galaxies, the Earth, land, volcanoes, fountains in the deep oceans, flowers, in the different types of animals, and in the organisms that battle inside of our bodies. All of creation screams God exists! Also, it is undisputed that Jesus Christ walked this Earth, so we know that He existed in the flesh. We also know that He claimed to be the Son of God and God. We also know that He performed righteous miracles and taught with Godly wisdom. Jesus Christ came to do many things, but one was to testify to the truth. We have preserved copies of His Words and witness testimonies of people who walked with Him, and people who received the Holy Spirit after He resurrected and then testified about Him!

The Old Testament tells us of the old covenant that God made with His people, and the New Testament tells us of the new covenant that God made with all of those who place their trust in Christ and follow Him. We see in the Old Testament how man could not meet the righteous standards of God, due the fall of humanity through the sins of our ancestors Adam and Eve. We see how Levitical priests sacrificed animals to atone for the sins of God's people.[30]

In the New Testament, we see God born in the flesh and humbling Himself to be the final sacrifice to atone for the sins of those who trust and follow Him! It is amazing that we have a holy, righteous, powerful, loving, and merciful God who made a way for sinners!

We know that Jesus Christ quoted scripture from the Old Testament thereby validating it while rebuking the religious leaders for their interpretation of some of the laws.

Also, here's an interesting fact. "The Old Testament is the part of the Bible written before Jesus was born. Its writings were completed in 450 B.C. The Old Testament, written hundreds of years before Jesus' birth, contains over 300 prophecies that Jesus fulfilled through His life, death and resurrection."[31]

For example, Isaiah 53 was written approximately hundreds of years before Jesus Christ's birth, and it is speaking of Him:

Who hath believed our report? and to whom is

the arm of the Lord revealed? For he shall grow

up before him as a tender plant, and as a root out

---

[30] https://www.gotquestions.org/Levitical-priesthood.html
[31] http://www1.cbn.com/biblestudy/biblical-prophecies-fulfilled-by-jesus

of a dry ground: he hath no form nor comeliness; and when we shall see him, there is no beauty that we should desire him. He is despised and rejected of men; a man of sorrows, and acquainted with grief: and we hid as it were our faces from him; he was despised, and we esteemed him not. **Surely he hath borne our griefs, and carried our sorrows: yet we did esteem him stricken, smitten of God, and afflicted. But he was wounded for our transgressions, he was bruised for our iniquities: the chastisement of our peace was upon him; and with his stripes we are healed. All we like sheep have gone astray; we have turned every one to his own way; and the Lord hath laid on him the iniquity of us all. He was oppressed, and he was afflicted, yet he opened not his mouth: he is brought as a lamb to the slaughter, and as a sheep before her shearers is dumb, so he openeth not his mouth. He was taken from prison and from judgment: and who shall declare his generation? for he was cut off out of the land of the living: for the transgression of my people was he stricken. And he made his grave with the wicked, and with the rich in his death;**

because he had done no violence, neither was any deceit in his mouth. Yet it pleased the Lord to bruise him; he hath put him to grief: when thou shalt make his soul an offering for sin, he shall see his seed, he shall prolong his days, and the pleasure of the Lord shall prosper in his hand. He shall see of the travail of his soul, and shall be satisfied: by his knowledge shall my righteous servant justify many; for he shall bear their iniquities. Therefore will I divide him a portion with the great, and he shall divide the spoil with the strong; because he hath poured out his soul unto death: **and he was numbered with the transgressors; and he bare the sin of many, and made intercession for the transgressors.** Isaiah 53 KJV [Emphasis Added]

Also, we can study the Dead Sea Scrolls and the New Testament manuscripts online.[32] In addition to the preserved copies of witness testimonies, we have proof that Jesus Christ still changes lives! What all Christians know is that the truth sets a man or woman free. Therefore, I am providing a list of important truths that I learned before and after giving my life

---

[32] https://www.deadseascrolls.org.il/explore-the-archive?locale=en%20US and http://www.csntm.org/

to Christ! It is important for me to explain that I oppose *false teachings* in any religion, or any denomination. Most of my family and friends are Catholic, and I love them dearly, so please know that I love all people! I do disagree with the doctrine being taught by the Vatican, the occult, and the protestant churches that contradict biblical teachings. Therefore, some of what I learned may offend some, but the false doctrine was preventing me and others from finding the saving truth; Jesus Christ!

In order to keep it simple, most scripture verses will be in block quotes, even if they have less than three lines of text.

<u>Jesus Christ is the Only Way to the Father</u>.

We are not saved by works of the law or by man-made sacraments. I learned that we must repent of self-rule and sins. The Holy Spirit gives us the ability to repent and do good works. We cannot do that on our own. We cannot "be good enough" and earn our salvation. The Bible says we all fall short of His holiness, which is why we need Jesus Christ to be the propitiation for our sins.

> Jesus said to him, I am the way, and the truth, and the life. No one comes to the Father except through me. *John 14:6 ESV*

> In the beginning was the Word, and the Word was with God, and the Word was God. He was in the beginning with God. All things were made through him, and without him was not any thing

made that was made. In him was life, and the life was the light of men. The light shines in the darkness, and the darkness has not overcome it. There was a man sent from God, whose name was John. He came as a witness, to bear witness about the light, that all might believe through him. He was not the light, but came to bear witness about the light. The true light, which gives light to everyone, was coming into the world. He was in the world, and the world was made through him, yet the world did not know him. He came to his own, and his own people did not receive him. But to all who did receive him, who believed in his name, he gave the right to become children of God, who were born, not of blood nor of the will of the flesh nor of the will of man, but of God. And the Word became flesh and dwelt among us, and we have seen his glory, glory as of the only Son from the Father, full of grace and truth. (John bore witness about him, and cried out, "This was he of whom I said, 'He who comes after me ranks before me, because he was before me.'") For from his fullness we have all received, grace upon grace. For the law was given through Moses; grace and truth came through Jesus Christ. No one has ever seen God; the only God, who is at the Father's side, he has made him known. John 1:1-18 ESV

For by works of the law no human being will be justified in his sight, since through the law comes knowledge of sin. Romans 3:20 ESV **[Emphasis added]**

What then? Are we Jews any better off? No, not at all. For we have already charged that all, both Jews and Greeks, are under sin, as it is written: "None is righteous, no, not one; no one understands; no one seeks for God. Romans 3:9-10 ESV

for all have sinned and fall short of the glory of God, and **are justified by his grace as a gift, through the redemption that is in Christ Jesus,** whom God put forward as a propitiation by his blood, **to be received by faith.** This was to show God's righteousness, because in his divine forbearance he had passed over former sins. **It was to show his righteousness at the present time, so that he might be just and the justifier of the one who has faith [trust] in Jesus.** Then what becomes of our boasting? It is excluded. By what kind of law? By a law of works? No, but by the law of faith. For we hold that one is justified by faith apart from works of the law. Or is God the God of Jews only? Is he not the God of Gentiles also? Yes, of Gentiles also, since God is one—who will justify the circumcised by faith and the uncircumcised through faith. Do we then overthrow the law by this faith? By no means! On the contrary, we uphold the law. Romans 3:23-31 ESV [Emphasis added]

But God, being rich in mercy, because of the great love with which he loved us, even when we were dead in our trespasses, made us alive together with Christ—**by grace you have been saved**—and raised us up with him and seated us with him in the heavenly places in Christ Jesus, so that in the coming ages he might show the immeasurable riches of his grace in kindness toward us in Christ Jesus. **For by grace you have been saved through faith. And this is not your own doing; it is the gift of God, not a result of works, so that no one may boast.** For we are his workmanship, created in Christ Jesus for good works, which God prepared beforehand, that we should walk in them. Ephesians 2:4-9 ESV [Emphasis added]

> For by works of the law no human being will be
> justified in his sight, since through the law comes
> knowledge of sin. Romans 3:20 ESV

<u>Salvation is Not Just Believing in His Existence</u>.
Before, I only had blind faith in Jesus Christ's existence and not a saving trust that included turning from self-rule to wanting to follow Christ. John 3:16 ESV states:

> For God so loved the world, that he gave his only
> begotten Son, that whosoever believeth in him
> should not perish, but have everlasting life.

According to the e-sword King James Version with Strong's Numbers, the word "believeth" in this verse is translated from the Greek word "pisteuo," which means *"to have faith (in, upon, or with respect to, a person or thing), that is, credit; by implication to entrust (especially one's spiritual well being to Christ): - believe (-r), commit (to trust), put in trust with."*

Therefore, faith is trusting Jesus Christ, and we cannot trust Him if we do not know His teachings. Even the demons believe in His existence. Some demons will pretend to be Jesus Christ or the Holy Spirit, so we must know the Word of God to test what thought or doctrine is coming from God.

You believe that God is one; you do well. Even the demons believe – and shudder! James 2:19 ESV

Then said Jesus unto his disciples, If any man will come after me, let him deny himself, and take up his cross, and follow me. For whosoever will save his life shall lose it: and whosoever will lose his life for my sake shall find it. For what is a man profited, if he shall gain the whole world, and lose his own soul? or what shall a man give in exchange for his soul? Matthew 16:24-26 KJV

According to www.bibleinfo.com:

But it also speaks of Jesus as "the Christ," meaning "the anointed one," the Messiah. When Jesus asked His disciples who they thought He was, Peter answered, "You are the Christ, the Son of the living God" (Matthew 16:16). At Jesus' interrogation by the Jews just before His crucifixion, the high priest demanded, "Tell us if You are the Christ, the Son of God!" (Matthew 26:63).

Luke records that one occasion when Jesus cast demons out of individuals, the demons cried out, 'You are the Christ, the Son of God!' and He [Jesus]

rebuking them, did not allow them to speak, for they knew that He was the Christ. (Luke 4:41)."[33]

Jesus Christ Had Authority to Lay Down His Life and Take it Up.

So Jesus again said to them, "Truly, truly, I say to you, **I am the door of the sheep**. All who came before me are thieves and robbers, but the sheep did not listen to them. I am the door. **If anyone enters by me, he will be saved and will go in and out and find pasture.** The thief comes only to steal and kill and destroy. I came that they may have life and have it abundantly. I am the good shepherd. The good shepherd lays down his life for the sheep. He who is a hired hand and not a shepherd, who does not own the sheep, sees the wolf coming and leaves the sheep and flees, and the wolf snatches them and scatters them. He flees because he is a hired hand and cares nothing for the sheep. I am the good shepherd. I know my own and my own know me, just as the Father knows me and I know the Father; and I lay down my life for the sheep. And I have other sheep that are not of this fold. I must bring them also, and

---

[33] https://www.bibleinfo.com/en/questions/what-does-christ-mean

they will listen to my voice. So there will be one flock, one shepherd. For this reason the Father loves me, because I lay down my life that I may take it up again. No one takes it from me, but I lay it down of my own accord. I have authority to lay it down, and I have authority to take it up again. This charge I have received from my Father. John 10:7-18 ESV [Emphasis Added]

Jesus Christ is the High Priest and Mediator Who Makes Intercession for Sinners.

This makes Jesus the guarantor of a better covenant. The former priests were many in number, because they were prevented by death from continuing in office, but he holds his priesthood permanently, because he continues forever. Consequently, he [Jesus] is able to save to the uttermost those who draw near to God through him, since he always lives to make intercession for them. For it was indeed fitting that we should have such a high priest, holy, innocent, unstained, separated from sinners, and exalted above the heavens. He has no need, like those high priests, to offer sacrifices daily, first for his own sins and then for those of the people, since he did this once for all when he offered up himself. For the law appoints men in their weakness as high priests, but the word of the oath, which came later than the law, appoints a Son **who has been made perfect forever.** Hebrews 7:22-28 ESV [Emphasis added]

Therefore he [Jesus] is the mediator of a new covenant, so that those who are called may receive the promised eternal inheritance, since a death has occurred that redeems them from the transgressions committed under the first covenant. Hebrews 9:15 ESV

For through him [Jesus Christ] we both have access by one Spirit unto the Father. Now therefore ye are no more strangers and foreigners, but fellowcitizens with the saints, and of the household of God; And are built upon the foundation of the apostles and prophets, Jesus Christ himself being the chief corner stone; In whom all the building fitly framed together groweth unto an holy temple in the Lord: Ephesians 2:18-21 ESV

For there is one God, and one mediator between God and men, the man Christ Jesus; Who gave himself a ransom for all, to be testified in due time. 1 Timothy 2:5-6 KJV

But now hath he obtained a more excellent ministry, by how much also he is the mediator of a better covenant, which was established upon better promises. For if that first covenant had been faultless, then should no place have been sought for the second. For finding fault with them, he saith, Behold, the days come, saith the Lord, when I will make a new covenant with the house of Israel and with the house of Judah: Not according to the covenant that I made with their fathers in the day when I took them by the hand to lead them out of the land of Egypt; because they continued not in my covenant, and I regarded them not, saith the Lord. For this is the covenant that I will make with the house of Israel after those days, saith the Lord; I will put my laws into their mind, and write them in their hearts: and I will be to them a God, and they shall be to me a people: And they shall not teach every man his neighbour, and every man his brother, saying, Know the Lord: for all shall know me, from the least to the greatest. For I will be merciful to their unrighteousness, and their sins and their iniquities will I remember no more. In that he saith, A new covenant, he hath made the first old.

Now that which decayeth and waxeth old is ready to vanish away. Hebrews 8:6-13 KJV

Wherefore then serveth the law? It was added because of transgressions, till the seed should come to whom the promise was made; and it was ordained by angels in the hand of a mediator. Now a mediator is not a mediator of one, but God is one. Is the law then against the promises of God? God forbid: for if there had been a law given which could have given life, verily righteousness should have been by the law. But the scripture hath concluded all under sin, that the promise by faith of Jesus Christ might be given to them that believe. But before faith came, we were kept under the law, shut up unto the faith which should afterwards be revealed. Wherefore the law was our schoolmaster to bring us unto Christ, that we might be justified by faith. But after that faith is come, we are no longer under a schoolmaster. For ye are all the children of God by faith in Christ Jesus. For as many of you as have been baptized into Christ have put on Christ. There is neither Jew nor Greek, there is neither bond nor free, there is neither male nor female: for ye are all one in Christ Jesus. **And if ye be**

Christ's, then are ye Abraham's seed, and heirs according to the promise. Galatians 3:19-29 KJV [Emphasis Added]

And for this cause he is the mediator of the new testament, that by means of death, for the redemption of the transgressions that were under the first testament, they which are called might receive the promise of eternal inheritance. For where a testament is, there must also of necessity be the death of the testator. Hebrews 9:15-16 KJV

The Veil in The Temple Tore - Earthly Priests No Longer Atone for People's Sins.

And Jesus cried again with a loud voice, and yielded up his spirit. **And behold, the veil of the temple was rent in two from the top to the bottom;** and the earth did quake; and the rocks were rent; Matthew 27:50-51 ASV [Emphasis Added]

For he is our peace, who made both one, and brake down the middle wall of partition, having abolished in his flesh the enmity, even the law of commandments contained in ordinances; that he might create in himself of the two one new man, so making peace; and might reconcile them both in one **body unto God through the cross, having slain the enmity thereby: and he came and preached peace to you that were far off, and peace to them that were nigh; for through him we both have our access in one Spirit unto the Father.** So then ye are no more strangers and sojourners, **but ye are fellow-citizens with the saints, and of the household of God, being built upon the foundation of the apostles and prophets, Christ Jesus himself being the chief corner stone**; in whom each several building, fitly framed together, groweth into a holy temple in the Lord; **in whom ye also are builded together for a habitation of God in the Spirit.** Ephesians 2:14-22 ASV [Emphasis Added]

<u>The Will of God</u>.

Jesus taught us that we are part of His family if we do the will of His Father.

And one said until him, 'Behold thy mother and thy brethren stand without, seeking to speak to thee.' But he answered and said unto him that told him, 'Who is my mother? And who are my brethren?' And he stretched forth his hand towards his disciples, and said, 'Behold, my mother and my brethren! **For whosoever shall do**

the will of my Father who is in heaven, he is my brother, and sister, and mother.' Matthew 12:47-50 ASV [Emphasis added]

But seek ye first the kingdom of God, and his righteousness; and all these things shall be added unto you. Matthew 6:3 KJV

<u>Obeying Jesus Christ is Wise</u>.

Everyone then who hears these words of mine and does them will be like a wise man who built his house on the rock. And the rain fell, and the floods came, and the winds blew and beat on that house, but it did not fall, because it had been founded on the rock. Matthew 7:24-25 ESV

<u>Jesus Christ Wants a Relationship With Us</u>.

He wants to have a relationship with us, and our prayer life keeps us in communication with Him. Again, He tells us how to pray. Jesus said:

I am the true vine, and my Father is the husbandman. Every branch in me that beareth not fruit he taketh away: and every branch that beareth fruit, he purgeth it, that it may bring forth more fruit. Now ye are clean through the word which I have spoken unto you. Abide in me, and I in you. As the branch cannot bear fruit of itself, except it abide in the vine; no more can ye, except ye abide in me. I am the vine, ye are the branches: **He that abideth in me, and I in him, the same bringeth forth much fruit: for without me ye can do nothing.** If a man abide not in me, he is cast forth as a branch, and is withered; and men gather them, and cast them into the fire, and they are burned. **If ye abide in me, and my words abide in you, ye shall ask what ye will, and it shall be done unto you.** Herein is my Father glorified, that ye bear much fruit; so shall ye be my disciples. As the Father hath loved me, so have I loved you: continue ye in my love. If ye keep my commandments, ye shall abide in my love; even as I have kept my Father's commandments, and abide in his love. These things have I spoken unto you, that my joy might remain in you, and that your joy might be full. This is my commandment, That ye love one another, as I have loved you. Greater love hath no man than this, that a man lay down his life for his friends. Ye are my friends, if ye do whatsoever I command you. Henceforth I call you not servants; for the servant knoweth not what his lord doeth: but I have called you friends; for all things that I have heard of my

Father I have made known unto you. **Ye have not chosen me, but I have chosen you, and ordained you, that ye should go and bring forth fruit, and that your fruit should remain: that whatsoever ye shall ask of the Father in my name, he may give it you.**" John 15:1-16 KJV [Emphasis Added]

And in that day ye shall ask me nothing. Verily, verily, I say unto you, Whatsoever ye shall ask the Father in my name, he will give it you. Hitherto have ye asked nothing in my name: ask, and ye shall receive, that your joy may be full. These things have I spoken unto you in proverbs: but the time cometh, when I shall no more speak unto you in proverbs, but I shall shew you plainly of the Father. At that day ye shall ask in my name: and I say not unto you, that I will pray the Father for you: For the Father himself loveth you, because ye have loved me, and have believed that I came out from God. I came forth from the Father, and am come into the world: again, I leave the world, and go to the Father. John 16:23-28 KJV

And whatsoever ye shall ask in my name, that will I do, that the Father may be glorified in the Son.

If ye shall ask anything in my name, that will I do. John 14:13-14 ASV

Jesus Christ said, "Again I say unto you, That if two of you shall agree on earth as touching any thing that they shall ask, it shall be done for them of my Father which is in heaven. For where two or three are gathered together in my name, there am I in the midst of them." Matthew 18:19-20 KJV

If any of you lack wisdom, <u>let him ask of God</u>, that giveth to all men liberally, and upbraideth not; and it shall be given him. But let him ask in faith, nothing wavering. For he that wavereth is like a wave of the sea driven with the wind and tossed. James 1:5-6 KJV [Emphasis added]

<u>Priests Are Those Who Have Received the Holy Spirit</u>.

Apostle Peter said:

But you are a chosen race, a royal priesthood, a holy nation, a people for his own possession, that you may proclaim the excellencies of him who called you out of darkness into his marvelous light. Once you were not a people, but now you are God's people; once you had not received mercy, but now you have received mercy.

Beloved, I urge you as sojourners and exiles to abstain from the passions of the flesh, which wage war against your soul. Keep your conduct among the Gentiles honorable, so that when they speak against you as evildoers, they may see your good deeds and glorify God on the day of visitation. 1 Peter 2 9-10 ESV

The Bible (Word of God) is the Sole Authority and Source of Truth.

For the **word of God** is living and active, sharper than any two-edged sword, piercing to the division of soul and of spirit, of joints and of marrow, and discerning the thoughts and intentions of the heart. Hebrews 4:12 ESV [Emphasis added]

Now the parable is this: The seed [spiritual food] is the word of God. The ones along the path are those who have heard; then the devil comes and takes away the word from their hearts, so that they may not believe and be saved. And the ones on the rock are those who, when they hear the word, receive it with joy. But these have no root; they believe for a while, and in time of testing fall away. And as for what fell among the thorns, they are those who hear, but as they go on their way they are choked by the cares and riches and pleasures of life, and their fruit does not mature. As for that in the good soil, they are those who, hearing the word, hold it fast in an honest and good heart, and bear fruit with patience. Luke 8:11-15 ESV

But he answered and said, It is written, Man shall not live by bread alone, but by every word that proceedeth out of the mouth of God. Matthew 4:4 KJV

Sanctify them through thy truth: thy word is truth. John 17:17 KJV

<u>Tradition.</u>

I found that unbiblical traditions and philosophies of men, which contradict or oppose God, were rebuked by Jesus Christ.

Then Pharisees and scribes came to Jesus from Jerusalem and said, "Why do your disciples break the tradition of the elders? For they do not wash their hands when they eat." **He [Jesus] answered them, "And why do you break the commandment of God for the sake of your tradition?** For God commanded, 'Honor your father and your mother,' and, 'Whoever reviles father or mother must surely die.' But you say, 'If anyone tells his father or his mother, "What you would have gained from me is given to God, "he need not honor his father.' **So for the sake of your tradition you have made void the word of God.** You hypocrites! **Well did Isaiah prophesy of you, when he said: "'This people honors me with their lips, but their heart is far from me; in vain do they worship me, teaching as doctrines the commandments of men.'** Matthew 15:1-9 ESV [Emphasis added]

<u>Old Covenant vs. New Covenant</u>.

But as it is, **Christ has obtained a ministry that is as much more excellent than the old as the covenant he mediates is better, since it is enacted on better promises.** For if that first covenant had been faultless, there would have been no occasion to look for a second. For he finds fault with them when he says: **Behold, the days are coming, declares the Lord, when I will establish a new covenant with the house of Israel and with the house of Judah [Jesus Christ came through the Tribe of Judah – so those who trust and follow Him are adopted into the Tribe of Judah]**, not like the covenant that I made with their fathers on the day when I took them by the hand to bring them out of the land of Egypt. For they did not continue in my covenant, and so I showed no concern for them, declares the Lord. For this is the covenant that I will make with the house of Israel after those days, declares the Lord: **I will put my laws into their minds, and write them on their hearts, and I will be their God, and they shall be my people. And they shall not teach, each one his neighbor and each one his brother, saying, 'Know the Lord,' for they shall all know me, from the least of them to the greatest. For I will be merciful toward their iniquities, and I will remember their sins no more. In speaking of a new covenant, he makes the first one obsolete. And what is becoming obsolete and growing old is ready to vanish away.** Hebrews 8:6-13 ESV [Emphasis added]

[Y]et we know that a person is not justified by works of the law but through faith in Jesus Christ, so we also have believed in Christ Jesus, in order to be justified by faith in Christ and not by works of the law, because by works of the law no one will be justified. Galatians 2:16 ESV

I have been crucified with Christ. It is no longer I who live, but Christ who lives in me. And the life I now live in the flesh I live by faith in the Son of God, who loved me and gave himself for me. I do not nullify the grace of God, **for if righteousness were through the law, then Christ died for no purpose.** Galatians 2:20-21 ESV [Emphasis added]

<u>We Must Repent.</u>

Repentance precedes salvation. We cannot follow Christ without the Holy Spirit helping us turn (repent) from following ourselves first, so we should pray for our salvation. Also, the Holy Spirit can open our spiritual eyes and ears before He indwells a believer, so He helps us see where we were once blind. He also empowers us to follow Christ.

And he saith unto them, **Follow me,** and I will make you fishers of men. Matthew 4:19 KJV [Emphasis added]

Then Jesus told his disciples, "If anyone would come after me, let him deny himself and take up his cross and follow me. For whoever would save his life will lose it, but whoever loses his life for my sake will find it. For what will it profit a man if he gains the whole world and forfeits his soul? Or what shall a man give in return for his soul? Matthew 16:24-26 ESV [Emphasis added]

If any man serve me, let him follow me; and where I am, there shall also my servant be: if any man serve me, **him will my Father honour.** John 12:26 KJV [Emphasis added]

Whoever loves father or mother more than me is not worthy of me, and whoever loves son or daughter more than me is not worthy of me. **And whoever does not take his cross and follow me is not worthy of me. Whoever finds his life will lose it, and whoever loses his life for my sake will find it.** Matthew 10:37-39 ESV [Emphasis added]

Jesus says:

And saying, The time is fulfilled, and the kingdom of God is at hand: **repent ye, and believe the gospel.** Mark 1:15 KJV [Emphasis Added]

Apostle Peter said:

The Lord is not slack concerning his promise, as some men count slackness; but is longsuffering to us-ward, not willing that any should perish, **but that all should come to repentance.** 2 Peter 3:9 KJV [Emphasis Added]

Then Peter said unto them, Repent, and be baptized every one of you in the name of Jesus Christ for the remission of sins, and ye shall receive the gift of the Holy Ghost. Acts 2:38 KJV

Repent ye therefore, and be converted, that your sins may be blotted out, when the times of refreshing shall come from the presence of the Lord; And he shall send Jesus Christ, which before was preached unto you: Acts 3:19 KJV

<u>Praying to the Father in Jesus Christ's Name and Confessing Sin</u>.

The "Our Father" prayer says so much. We can see that Christ asked us to pray to the Father. We also see that we ask the Father to *"forgive us our debts," so we know that we are to confess our sins directly to God. If we at some point "confess [our] faults one to another, and pray one for another, that [we] may be healed,"* (James 5:16 KJV) then that is biblical for healing, but we still confess our sins directly to God. We also see that we are to pray that His "will be done in earth," and that He wants to deliver us from walking into temptation and evil.

After this manner therefore pray ye: **Our Father which art in heaven**, Hallowed be thy name. Thy kingdom come. Thy will be done in earth, as it is in heaven. Give us this day our daily bread. **And**

forgive us our debts, as we forgive our debtors. And lead us not into temptation, but deliver us from evil: For thine is the kingdom, and the power, and the glory, for ever. Amen. **For if ye forgive men their trespasses, your heavenly Father will also forgive you: But if ye forgive not men their trespasses, neither will your Father forgive your trespasses.** Matthew 6:9-15 ASV **[Emphasis added]**

Jesus Christ said, "And whatsoever ye shall ask in my name, that will I do, that the Father may be glorified in the Son. If ye shall ask any thing in my name, I will do it. If ye love me, keep my commandments. And I will pray the Father, and he shall give you another Comforter, that he may abide with you for ever; John 14:13-16 KJV

Jesus Christ said, "But thou, when thou prayest, enter into thy closet, and when thou hast shut thy door, **pray to thy Father** which is in secret; and thy Father which seeth in secret shall reward thee openly. **But when ye pray, use not vain repetitions,** as the heathen do: for they think that they shall be heard for their much speaking. Be not ye therefore like unto them: for your Father knoweth what things ye have need of, before ye ask him. Matthew 6:6-8 KJV [Emphasis added]

And I say unto you, Ask, and it shall be given you; seek, and ye shall find; knock, and it shall be opened unto you. For every one that asketh receiveth; and he that seeketh findeth; and to him that knocketh it shall be opened. If a son shall ask bread of any of you that is a father, will he give him a stone? or if he ask a fish, will he for a fish give him a serpent? Or if he shall ask an egg, will he offer him a scorpion? **If ye then, being evil, know how to give good gifts unto your children: how much more shall your heavenly Father give the Holy Spirit to them that ask him**? Luke 11:9 KJV [Emphasis Added]

Is anyone among you sick? **Let him call for the elders of the church, and let them pray over him,** anointing him with oil in the name of the Lord. And the prayer of faith will save the one who is sick, and the Lord will raise him up. And if he has committed sins, he will be forgiven. **Therefore, confess your sins to one another and pray for one another, that you may be healed. The prayer of a righteous person has great power as it is**

working. James 5:14-16 ESV [Emphasis Added]

For the eyes of the Lord are over the righteous, and **his ears are open unto their prayers**: but the face of the Lord is against them that do evil. 1 Peter 3:12 KJV [Emphasis Added]

<u>The Holy Spirit/Spiritual Baptism/Being Born Again.</u>

I received the Holy Spirit after I had repented and agreed to follow Christ. I found a church approximately a month later. I participated in water baptism about four months after I began going to church. The water baptism was the ceremony representing my decision to repent and follow Jesus Christ. Scripture says:

Therefore if any man be in Christ, **he is a new creature**: old things are passed away; behold, all things are become new. 2 Corinthians 5:17 KJV [Emphasis Added]

Jesus answered him, "Truly, truly, I say to you, unless one is born again he cannot see the kingdom of God." Nicodemus said to him, "How can a man be born when he is old? Can he enter a second time into his mother's womb and be born?" Jesus answered, "Truly, truly, I say to you, unless one is **born of water and the Spirit**, he cannot enter the kingdom of God. That which is born of the flesh is flesh, and that which is born of the Spirit is spirit. Do not marvel that I said to you, 'You must be born again.' The wind blows where it wishes, and you hear its sound, but you do not know where it comes from or where it goes. So it is with everyone who is born of the Spirit." John 3:3-8 ESV [Emphasis Added]

In him you also, **when you heard the word of truth, the gospel of your salvation, and believed in him, were sealed with the promised Holy Spirit**, who is the guarantee of our inheritance until we acquire possession of it, to the praise of his glory. Ephesians 1:13 ESV [Emphasis Added]

But the Comforter, which is the Holy Ghost, whom the Father will send in my name, he shall teach you all things, and bring all things to your remembrance, whatsoever I have said unto you. John 14:26 KJV

Then Peter said unto them, Repent, and be baptized every one of you in the name of Jesus Christ for the remission of sins, and ye shall receive the gift of the Holy Ghost. For the promise is unto you, and to your children, and to all that are afar off, even as many as the Lord our

God shall call. And with many other words did he testify and exhort, saying, Save yourselves from this untoward generation. Then they that gladly received his word were baptized: and the same day there were added unto them about three thousand souls. Acts 2:38-41 KJV [Emphasis added]

The Apostle Peter said:

And as I began to speak, the Holy Ghost fell on them, as on us at the beginning. Then remembered I the word of the Lord, how that he said, **John indeed baptized with water; but ye shall be baptized with the Holy Ghost.** Acts 11:15-16 KJV [Emphasis added]

The Apostle Peter said:

And after there had been much debate, Peter stood up and said to them, "Brothers, you know that in the early days God made a choice among you, that by my mouth the Gentiles should hear the word of the gospel and believe. And God, who knows the heart, bore witness to them, by giving them the Holy Spirit just as he did to us, and he made no distinction between us and them, having cleansed their hearts by faith. Now, therefore, why are you putting God to the test by placing a yoke on the neck of the disciples that neither our fathers nor we have been able to bear? **But we believe that we will be saved through the grace of the Lord Jesus, just as they will.** Acts 15:7-11 ASV [Emphasis added]

John the Baptist said:

John answered them all, saying, "I baptize you with water, but he who is mightier than I [Jesus Christ] is coming, the strap of whose sandals I am not worthy to untie. **He will baptize you with the Holy Spirit and fire.** Luke 3:16 ESV [Emphasis added]

Jesus Christ said to His disciples:

Go therefore and make disciples of all nations, baptizing them in the name of the Father and of the Son and of the Holy Spirit **teaching them to observe all that I have commanded you.** And behold, I am with you always, to the end of the age. Matthew 28:19 ESV [Emphasis added]

<u>The Holy Spirit and the Christian's Body</u>.

Our bodies are temples of the Holy Spirit. The Holy Spirit is God. He is a Person (not a force).

Know ye not that ye are the temple of God, and that the Spirit of God dwelleth in you? If any man defile the temple of God, him shall God destroy; for the temple of God is holy, which temple ye are. 1 Corinthians 3:16-17 KJV

What? know ye not that your body is the temple of the Holy Ghost which is in you, which ye have of God, and ye are not your own? 1 Corinthians 6:19 KJV

Know ye not that your bodies are the members of Christ? shall I then take the members of Christ, and make them the members of an harlot? God forbid. What? know ye not that he which is joined to an harlot is one body? for two, saith he, shall be one flesh. But he that is joined unto the Lord is one spirit. Flee fornication. Every sin that a man doeth is without the body; but he that committeth fornication sinneth against his own body. What? know ye not that your body is the temple of the Holy Ghost which is in you, which ye have of God, and ye are not your own? 1 Corinthians 6:15-19 KJV

<u>Fruits of the Holy Spirit (Love, Joy, Peace, Longsuffering, Gentleness, Faith, Meekness)</u>.

This I say then, Walk in the Spirit, and ye shall not fulfil the lust of the flesh. For the flesh lusteth against the Spirit, and the Spirit against the flesh: and these are contrary the one to the other: so that ye cannot do the things that ye would. **But if ye be led of the Spirit, ye are not under the law.** Now the works of the flesh are manifest, which are these; Adultery, fornication, uncleanness, lasciviousness, Idolatry, witchcraft, hatred, variance, emulations, wrath, strife, seditions, heresies, Envyings, murders, drunkenness, revellings, and such like: of the which I tell you before, as I have also told you in time past, that they which do such things shall not inherit the kingdom of God. **But the fruit of the Spirit is love, joy, peace, longsuffering, gentleness, goodness, faith, Meekness, temperance: against such there is no law.** And they that are Christ's have crucified the flesh with the affections and lusts. If we live in the Spirit, let us also walk in the Spirit. Let us not be desirous of vain glory, provoking one another, envying one another. Galatians 5:16-26 KJV [Emphasis Added]

<u>Sanctification.</u>

We are sanctified by the Holy Spirit through truth and the Word of God. The definition of sanctification is as follows:

> <u>Sanctification.</u> The biblical meaning of sanctification is "**1:** to set apart to a sacred purpose or to religious use :consecrate **2:** to free from sin: purify **3a:** to impart or impute sacredness, inviolability, or respect to **b:** to give moral or social sanction to **4:** to make productive of holiness or piety observe the day of the sabbath, to *sanctify* it — Deuteronomy 5:12 (Douay Version)"[34]
>
> Sanctify them in the truth; your word is truth. John 17:17 ESV [Emphasis added]
>
> But we ought always to give thanks to God for you, brothers beloved by the Lord, because God chose you as the firstfruits to be saved, **through sanctification by the Spirit and belief in the truth.** 2 Thessalonians 2:13 ESV [Emphasis added]
>
> I am speaking in human terms, because of your natural limitations. For just as you once

---

[34] https://www.merriam-webster.com/dictionary/sanctify

presented your members as slaves to impurity and to lawlessness leading to more lawlessness, so now present your members **as slaves to righteousness leading to sanctification**. Romans 6:19 ESV [Emphasis added]

<u>Witchcraft, the Occult, Familiar Spirits</u>.

Regard not them that have familiar spirits, neither seek after wizards, to be defiled by them: I am the LORD your God. Leviticus 19:31 KJV

And when they shall say unto you, Seek unto them that have familiar spirits and unto the wizards, that chirp and that mutter: **should not a people seek unto their God**? on behalf of the living should they seek unto the dead? Isaiah 8:19-20 ASV [Emphasis added]

<u>Items Do Not Protect or Save</u>.

Items (rocks, sticks, statutes, crosses, crucifixes, holy water, rosaries, and other items) do not protect us from the demonic or save us from spiritual death. Jesus Christ is the only One who can save and protect us. Reading or hearing the Word of God is what will lead people to a saving trust in Jesus Christ.

Assemble yourselves and come; draw near together, ye that are escaped of the nations: they have no knowledge that set up the wood of their graven image, and pray unto a god that cannot save. Tell ye, and bring them near; yea, let them take counsel together: who hath declared this from ancient time? who hath told it from that time? have not I the Lord? and there is no God else beside me; a just God and a Saviour; there is none beside me. Look unto me, and be ye saved, all the ends of the earth: for I am God, and there is none else. Isaiah 45:20-21 KJV

Christ-followers Are No Longer Slaves to Sin.

We are slaves to sin until Jesus Christ breaks the yoke. It is hard for Christ-followers to stay in sin because we are convicted by the Holy Spirit, and we now love God.

Jesus answered them, "Truly, truly, I say to you, everyone who practices sin is a slave to sin. The slave does not remain in the house forever; the son remains forever. **So if the Son sets you free, you will be free indeed.** John 8:34-36 ESV [Emphasis Added]

No one who abides in him keeps on sinning; no one who keeps on sinning has either seen him or known him. Little children, let no one deceive you. Whoever practices righteousness is righteous, as he is righteous. Whoever makes a practice of sinning is of the devil, for the devil has been sinning from the beginning. The reason the Son of God appeared was to destroy the works of the devil. 1 John 3:6-8 ESV [Emphasis Added]

<u>False Doctrine</u>.

Jesus Christ's Disciples Taught the First Churches (New Testament Churches) to Not Listen to False Doctrine.

But the Spirit saith expressly, that in later times some shall fall away from the faith, giving heed to seducing spirits and doctrines of demons, through the hypocrisy of men that speak lies, branded in their own conscience as with a hot iron; forbidding to marry, and commanding to abstain from meats, which God created to be received with thanksgiving by them that believe and know the truth. For every creature of God is good, and nothing is to be rejected, if it be received with thanksgiving: for it is sanctified through the word of God and prayer. If thou put the brethren in mind of these things, thou shalt be a good minister of Christ Jesus, nourished in the words of the faith, and of the good doctrine which thou hast followed until now: **but refuse profane and old wives' fables.** 1 Timothy 4:1-7 ASV [Emphasis added]

For a good tree bringeth not forth corrupt fruit; neither doth a corrupt tree bring forth good fruit. **For every tree is known by his own fruit. For of thorns men do not gather figs, nor of a bramble bush gather they grapes.** A good man out of the good treasure of his heart bringeth forth that which is good; and an evil man out of the evil treasure of his heart bringeth forth that which is evil: for of the abundance of the heart his mouth speaketh. And why call ye me, Lord, Lord, and do not the things which I say? Whosoever cometh to me, and heareth my sayings, and doeth them, I will shew you to whom he is like: He is like a man which built an house, and digged deep, and laid the foundation on a rock: and when the flood arose, the stream beat vehemently upon that house, and could not shake it: for it was founded upon a rock. But he that heareth, and doeth not, is like a man that without a foundation built an house upon the earth; against which the stream did beat vehemently, and immediately it fell; and the ruin of that house was great. Luke 6:43-49 KJV [Emphasis added]

Let no man deceive himself. If any man among you seemeth to be wise in this world, let him become a fool, that he may be wise. **For the wisdom of this world is foolishness with God.** For it is written, He taketh the wise in their own craftiness. **And again, The Lord knoweth the thoughts of the wise, that they are vain. Therefore let no man glory in men.** For all things are yours; Whether Paul, or Apollos, or Cephas, or the world, or life, or death, or things present, or things to come; all are yours; And ye are Christ's; and Christ is God's. 1 Corinthians 3:18-23 KJV [Emphasis added]

For the weapons of our warfare are not of the flesh but have divine power to destroy strongholds. **We destroy arguments and every lofty opinion raised against the knowledge of God, and take every thought captive to obey Christ.** 2 Corinthians 10:4-5 ESV [Emphasis added]

<u>False Teachers</u>.

Beware of false prophets, which come to you in sheep's clothing, but inwardly they are ravening wolves. Ye shall know them by their fruits. Do men gather grapes of thorns, or figs of thistles? Matthew 7:15-16 KJV

<u>Calling Others "Father."</u>

Then Jesus said to the crowds and to his disciples, "The scribes and the Pharisees sit on Moses' seat, so do and observe whatever they tell you, but not the works they do. For they preach, but do not practice. They tie up heavy burdens, hard to bear, and lay them on people's shoulders, but they themselves are not willing to move them with their finger. They do all their deeds to be seen by others. For they make their phylacteries broad and their fringes long, and they love the place of honor at feasts and the best seats in the synagogues and greetings in the marketplaces and being called rabbi by others. But you are not to be called rabbi, for you have one teacher, and you are all brothers. And call no man your father on earth, for you have one Father, **who is in heaven. Neither be called instructors, for you have one instructor, the Christ.** The greatest among you shall be your servant. Whoever exalts himself will be humbled, and whoever humbles himself will be exalted. "But woe to you, scribes and Pharisees, hypocrites! For you shut the kingdom of heaven in people's faces. For you neither enter yourselves nor allow those who would enter to go in. Woe to you, scribes and Pharisees, hypocrites! For you travel across sea and land to make a single proselyte, and when he becomes a proselyte, you make him twice as much a child of hell as yourselves. Matthew 23:1-15 ESV [Emphasis added]

<u>Hell</u>.

The gates of hell will not prevail against the spiritual Church, the Body of Christ. All those who have received the Holy Spirit are "the Church." Also, Jesus mentions an "everlasting punishment," not a sanctifying purgatory. We are sanctified through the Holy Spirit, the Word of God, and through doing the will of the Lord; this is biblical, as referenced before. Jesus said:

> And fear not them which kill the body, but are not able to kill the soul: but rather fear him which is able to destroy both soul and body in hell. Matthew 10:28 (KJV)

> And I say also unto thee, That thou art Peter, and upon this rock I will build my church; and the gates of hell shall not prevail against it. Matthew 16:18 (KJV)

> Ye serpents, ye generation of vipers, how can ye escape the damnation of hell? Matthew 23:33 (KJV)

Then shall he say also unto them on the left hand, Depart from me, ye cursed, into everlasting fire, prepared for the devil and his angels: For I was an hungred, and ye gave me no meat: I was thirsty, and ye gave me no drink: I was a stranger, and ye took me not in: naked, and ye clothed me not: sick, and in prison, and ye visited me not. Then shall they also answer him, saying, Lord, when saw we thee an hungred, or athirst, or a stranger, or naked, or sick, or in prison, and did not minister unto thee? Then shall he answer them, saying, Verily I say unto you, Inasmuch as ye did it not to one of the least of these, ye did it not to me. And these shall go away into everlasting punishment: but the righteous into life eternal." Matthew 25:44-46 (KJV)

Jesus also mentioned a "fire that never shall be quenched."

And if thy foot offend thee, cut it off: it is better for thee to enter halt into life, than having two feet to be cast into hell, into the fire that never shall be quenched: Mark 9:45 KJV

Jesus told this story about Hell:

There was a certain rich man, which was clothed in purple and fine linen, and fared sumptuously every day: And there was a certain beggar named Lazarus, which was laid at his gate, full of sores, And desiring to be fed with the crumbs which fell from the rich man's table: moreover the dogs came and licked his sores. And it came to pass, that the beggar died, and was carried by the angels into Abraham's bosom: the rich man also died, and was buried; And in hell he lift up his eyes, being in torments, and seeth Abraham afar off, and Lazarus in his bosom. And he cried and said, Father Abraham, have mercy on me, and send Lazarus, that he may dip the tip of his finger in water, and cool my tongue; for I am tormented in this flame. But Abraham said, Son, remember that thou in thy lifetime receivedst thy good things, and likewise Lazarus evil things: but now he is comforted, and thou art tormented. And beside all this, between us and you there is a great gulf fixed: so that they which would pass from hence to you cannot; neither can they pass to us, that would come from thence. Then he said, I pray thee therefore, father, that thou wouldest send him to my father's house: For I have five brethren; that he may testify unto them, lest they also come into this place of torment. Abraham saith unto him, They have Moses and the prophets; let them hear them. And he said, Nay, father Abraham: but if one went unto them from the dead, they will repent. And he said unto him, If they hear not Moses and the prophets, neither will they be persuaded, though one rose from the dead. Luke 16:19-31 KJV

<u>The Devil</u>.

The devil was cast down from Heaven. He is a deceiver and a liar. He will be tormented forever one day.

> And the great dragon was cast down, the old serpent, he that is called the Devil and Satan, the deceiver of the whole world; he was cast down to the earth, and his angels were cast down with him. Revelation 12:9 ASV

> You are of your father the devil, and your will is to do your father's desires. He was a murderer from the beginning, and does not stand in the truth, because there is no truth in him. When he lies, he speaks out of his own character, for he is a liar and the father of lies. John 8:44 ESV

> **[A]nd the devil who had deceived them was thrown in the lake of fire and sulfur where the beast and the false prophet were, and they will**

be tormented day and night forever and forever.
Revelation 20:10 ESV [Emphasis Added]

<u>Satan's Followers Can Perform Signs.</u>

We can learn from my story that people can hear deceiving voices and thoughts. We can also be deceived by signs and wonders. Dr. Carlin said, "A lie is as powerful as the truth if one believes it." We know that the Bible says that some who follow the devil will do signs and wonders. Therefore, we cannot believe that every sign or wonder is from God.

> For such are false apostles, deceitful workers, transforming themselves into the apostles of Christ. And no marvel; for Satan himself is transformed into an angel of light. Therefore it is no great thing if his ministers also be transformed as the ministers of righteousness; whose end shall be according to their works. 2 Corinthians 11:13-15 (KJV)

> Even him, whose coming is after the working of Satan with all power and signs and lying wonders. 2 Thessalonians 2:9 (KJV)

> And I beheld another beast coming up out of the earth; and he had two horns like a lamb, and he spake as a dragon. And he exerciseth all the power of the first beast before him, and causeth the earth and them which dwell therein to

worship the first beast, whose deadly wound was healed. And he doeth great wonders, so that he maketh fire come down from heaven on the earth in the sight of men, And deceiveth them that dwell on the earth by the means of those miracles which he had power to do in the sight of the beast; saying to them that dwell on the earth, that they should make an image to the beast, which had the wound by a sword, and did live. And he had power to give life unto the image of the beast, that the image of the beast should both speak, and cause that as many as would not worship the image of the beast should be killed. And he causeth all, both small and great, rich and poor, free and bond, to receive a mark in their right hand, or in their foreheads: And that no man might buy or sell, save he that had the mark, or the name of the beast, or the number of his name. Here is wisdom. Let him that hath understanding count the number of the beast: for it is the number of a man; and his number is Six hundred threescore and six. Rev 13:11-18 (KJV)

And the third angel followed them, saying with a loud voice, If any man worship the beast and his image, and receive his mark in his forehead, or in his hand, The same shall drink of the wine of the wrath of God, which is poured out without mixture into the cup of his indignation; and he shall be tormented with fire and brimstone in the presence of the holy angels, and in the presence of the Lamb: And the smoke of their torment ascendeth up for ever and ever: and they have no rest day nor night, who worship the beast and his image, and whosoever receiveth the mark of his name. Revelation 14:9-11 (KJV)

<u>Mary</u>.

Mary was obedient to God and is precious in His eyes. Some people worship Mary and believe that she is the mother to Jesus Christ in Heaven. However, there is not scripture to support that Mary is part of the Holy Trinity or that she is the mother of Jesus Christ in Heaven. There is plenty of scripture to support God's command to worship only Him.

In addition, Mary referenced God as her Savior. Some have said that she could not have been a sinner because she carried Jesus Christ in her womb. If she wasn't a sinner, then she wouldn't have referred to God as her Savior. Also, Christ-followers receive the Holy Spirit to live inside of their bodies, and the Holy Spirit is God, as well.

And Mary said, **"My soul magnifies the Lord, and my spirit rejoices in God my Savior**, for he has looked on the humble estate of his servant. For behold, from now on all generations will call me blessed; for he who is mighty has done great things for me, and holy is his name. Luke 1:46-49 ESV [Emphasis Added]

Know ye not that ye are the temple of God, and that the Spirit of God dwelleth in you? 1 Corinthians 3:16 KJV

Moreover, some believe that they are praying to Mary, but there is not scripture to support that praying to anyone other than God is biblical. Also, there is scripture saying that praying to the physically dead is forbidden. Also, there is not scripture to support that Mary, or any other Saint, can hear people's prayers. I talk about this more under "Praying to Saints in Heaven."

<u>Lady Fatima</u>.

Lady Fatima sounds nothing like the biblical Mary. Lady Fatima sought her own glory, which goes against all scripture in the Old Testament and the New Testament. According to Portugal.com, the entity who claims to be Lady Fatima said the following:

While she did not reveal her full name right away, the lady did tell the children: "I am of Heaven."

When asked, she promised that all three of the children would go to heaven, though Francisco would have to **say "many rosaries" in order to get there**.

For the second apparition on June 13, dozens of onlookers testified that they were able to see a cloud above the tree where the children saw Mary. This time, she showed the children her Immaculate Heart, pierced with thorns representing the sins of mankind.

Lucia asked Mary for the healing of a sick person, which Mary said would be granted with his conversion. Lucia again asked Mary to take the children to heaven, and while Mary promised to take Jacinta and Francisco soon, she told Lucia that she must stay on earth "some time longer.

Jesus wishes to make use of you to make me known and loved," Mary told her. "He wants to establish in the world devotion to my Immaculate Heart. I promise salvation to those who embrace it, and those souls will be loved by God like flowers placed by me to adorn His throne." [Emphasis Added]

She asked the children to help sinners by sacrificing themselves:

> **Sacrifice yourself for sinners**, and say many times, especially whenever you make some sacrifice: O my Jesus, it is for love of Thee, for the conversion of sinners, and **in reparation for the sins committed against the Immaculate Heart of Mary.**
>
> Mary again repeated her request for daily rosaries, and asked that a chapel be built at the apparition site **honoring the Lady of the Rosary, which she revealed to the children as her identity.**[35] [Emphasis Added.]

Lady Fatima wanted the children to tell Jesus Christ that their sacrifice was for the "conversion of sinners" which is unbiblical, as even the Old Testament priests could not sacrifice enough animals to convert someone. Further, Jesus Christ is the only one who was able to sacrifice Himself for sinners to atone for their sins because He is God, and He is sinless.

Lady Fatima made it appear as though Jesus Christ's sacrifice on the cross was not enough. Lady Fatima was also known to say, "Pray; pray very much. Make sacrifices for

---

[35] https://www.catholicnewsagency.com/news/everything-you-need-to-know-about-fatima-part-1-15388

sinners. Many souls go to hell because **no one is willing to help them with sacrifice**" and "God is pleased with your sacrifices, **but he does not want you to wear the cords [around your waists as a penance] to bed. Keep them on during the day**."[36]

She did not share the gospel "good news" of Jesus Christ, and she was not trying to make disciples of Christ, like Jesus Christ commanded when He said, *"Go ye therefore, and teach all nations, baptizing them in the name of the Father, and of the Son, and of the Holy Ghost:"* Matthew 28:19 KJV. Also, we can see from this verse that Jesus didn't mention anyone being baptized in Mary. Instead, Lady Fatima told the children that Jesus wanted her to be made "known and loved." If that's true, why is there nothing in the Bible to support that? Why didn't Jesus Christ mention that? He is the boss. He is God. He would have told His disciples that, but He did not.

She also said that sins were committed against her, not Him, and she promised salvation, but Jesus Christ said, *"Take heed lest any man deceive you; For many shall come in my name, saying, I am Christ; and shall deceive many."* Mark 13:5-6 KJV.

The English word "Christ" comes from the Hebrew word "Messiah." The Messiah is the One who saves from sin,

---

[36] http://www.ncregister.com/daily-news/marys-fatima-messages-to-the-shepherd-children

so if anyone else says that they are the one who saves from sin (promises salvation), then that one is claiming to be the Messiah, the Christ. Lady Fatima cannot offer salvation. Biblical Mary cannot offer salvation. Biblical Mary already acknowledged that God was her Savior. Salvation is a gift from God. *"For by grace you have been saved through faith. And this is not your own doing; it is the gift of God, not a result of works, so that no one may boast."* Ephesians 2:8-9 ESV

Further, biblical Mary never said that she could offer or promise salvation. The world was waiting on the Lord and Savior, who she carried in her womb, so that He could offer Himself as a punishment for the sins of those who place their trust in Him and follow Him. Jesus Christ said that He is the only way to the Father. He is the truth, the life, and the way. (John 14:6).

The first apostles, including Peter, never said that Mary could offer salvation or reconcile us to the Father. Scripture in the Old Testament points to Jesus Christ's coming, and scripture in the New Testament witnesses to His physical birth on Earth, His walk, His sinless life, His ministry, His miracles, His healings, His casting out of demons, His foretelling of His own Earthly death, His suffering and death, and His resurrection. The New Testament also testifies to the huge transformations that took place in disciples of Christ after they received the Holy

Spirit. We still see transformations today in those who have given their life to follow Jesus Christ.

Also, biblical Mary never asked anyone to sacrifice or punish themselves. Jesus Christ never asked us to punish ourselves. None of the first apostles asked anyone to punish themselves. Apostle Peter did not speak of any "penance" or punishment in his Letters in the New Testament.

The penance Lady Fatima required was adopted by the Roman Church; a penance, which usually involves reciting the prayer "Hail Mary" to "Lady Fatima." This entity would know that God commands us to worship and pray to only God, as His commands are clear throughout the Old and New Testaments.

Biblical Mary magnified the Lord and called Him her Lord and Savior. She never once sought to glorify herself. There is nothing in the Bible stating that God the Father or the Son or the Holy Spirit want Mary "to [be] known and loved...[and] establish in the world devotion to...[her] Immaculate Heart...[and have her] promise salvation to those who embrace it..." Christ said:

> I am the light of the world. Whoever follows me
> will not walk in darkness, but will have the light of
> life." John 8:12 ESV.

He also says:

> The thief comes to steal and kill and destroy. I came that they may have life and have it abundantly. I am the good shepherd. The good shepherd lays down his life for the sheep. John 10:10-11 ESV

To believe Lady Fatima over Jesus Christ would not be logical because He is God, He is the truth, and He made Himself and His teachings clear to us in scripture. Lady Fatima insinuates that what Jesus Christ did on the cross was not enough and that there is a new way to be saved. There's not. Lady Fatima didn't suffer and die on the cross for our sins. Biblical Mary didn't spend time punishing herself to save people.

Further, Jesus Christ never said that Mary was God. He never said that she could offer salvation or that she was the truth, the life, and the way.

Again, the biblical Mary would have sought to glorify God and point to Jesus Christ as Lord and Savior, just as recorded in scripture. Many of the voices deceived me into believing that they were someone else. Those deceiving entities, and others, will continue to deceive, which is why the Bible tells us to test every spirit, and we do this by using the Word of God.

Beloved, do not believe every spirit, but test the spirits to see whether they are from God, for many false prophets have gone out into the world. 1 John 4:1 ESV All scripture is given by inspiration of God, and is profitable for doctrine, for reproof, for correction, for instruction in righteousness: 2 Timothy 3:16 KJV For the word of God is quick, and powerful, and sharper than any twoedged sword, piercing even to the dividing asunder of soul and spirit, and of the joints and marrow, and is a discerner of the thoughts and intents of the heart. Hebrews 4:12 KJV

Also, Jesus Christ sought to glorify the Father. Jesus always sought to glorify the Father. Even when Jesus acknowledged that He Himself was God, and one with the Father, He still glorified the Father. Again, Jesus Christ never said that Mary was God, or the way to the Father.

Neither did the first apostles. Apostle Peter never said that Mary was the way to the Father, or someone we should pray to, or worship. Peter's letters are accessible in the New Testament, and his teachings line up with Jesus Christ's teachings.

Also, we are to worship only God. We are not supposed to bow down or kneel to any other man, woman, statute, rock, stick, or any other object.

> When Peter entered, Cornelius met him and fell down at his feet and worshiped him. But Peter lifted him up, saying, Stand up; I too am a man. Acts 10:25-26 ESV

The Bible says we all fall short (sin):

> the righteousness of God through faith in Jesus Christ for all who believe for there is no distinction: for all have sinned and fall short of the glory of God, and are justified by his grace as a gift, through the redemption that is in Christ Jesus, whom God put forward as a propitiation by his blood, to be received by faith. Romans 3:22-25 ESV [Emphasis Added]

Further, praying the rosary is asking those who are seeking the truth to obey Lady Fatima even though her doctrine does not line up with scripture in the Old or New Testaments. Again, the biblical Mary would tell us to magnify the Lord, not her, and to do what Jesus Christ commands us to do. Obedience to false doctrine gives the enemy access to influence our lives. Jesus said:

My sheep hear my voice, and I know them, and they **follow me**: John 10:27 KJV [Emphasis Added]

And I give unto them eternal life; and they shall never perish, neither shall any man pluck them out of my hand. John 10:28 KJV

My Father, which gave them me, **is greater than all**; and no man is able to pluck them out of my Father's hand. John 10:29 KJV [Emphasis Added]

I and my Father are one. John 10:30 KJV

God said: You shall have no other gods before me. Exodus 20:3 ESV

Also, it was said that Lady Fatima had appeared with the Child Jesus, but Christ already resurrected from the dead, and He is sitting at the right hand of the Father. Christ would not appear as a child and allow Lady Fatima to teach doctrine that ignores what He did on the cross.

Which he wrought in Christ, when he raised him from the dead, and set him at his own right hand in the heavenly places, Far above all principality, and power, and might, and dominion, and every name that is named, not only in this world, but also in that which is to come: And hath put all things under his feet, and gave him to be the head over all things to the church, Which is his body, the fulness of him that filleth all in all. Ephesians 1:20-23 KJV

Other Relevant Scripture Regarding False Gods and Testing Spirits.

Thou shalt not make unto thee any graven image, or any likeness of any thing that is in heaven above, or that is in the earth beneath, or that is in the water under the earth: Thou shalt not bow down thyself to them, nor serve them: for I the LORD thy God am a jealous God, visiting the iniquity of the fathers upon the children unto the third and fourth generation of them that hate me; And shewing mercy unto thousands of them that love me, and keep my commandments. Exodus 20:4-6 KJV [Emphasis Added.]

Yet ye have forsaken me, and served other gods: wherefore I will deliver you no more. Go and cry unto the gods which ye have chosen; let them deliver you in the time of your tribulation. Judges 10:13-14 KJV

And go not after other gods to serve them, and to worship them, and provoke me not to anger with the works of your hands; and I will do you no hurt. Jeremiah 25:6 KJV [Emphasis Added.]

<u>Saints</u>.

On earth, Saints are those who have the Holy Spirit in them.

> To the church of God that is in Corinth, to those sanctified in Christ Jesus, called to be saints together with all those who in every place call upon the name of our Lord Jesus Christ, both their Lord and ours: 1 Corinthians 1:2 ESV

> Paul and Timothy, servants of Christ Jesus, To all the saints in Christ Jesus who are at Philippi, with the overseers and deacons: Philippians 1:1 ESV

<u>Praying to Saints in Heaven</u>.

We are not supposed to pray to the dead. Not even the physically dead saints. There is nothing in scripture telling us that the Saints in Heaven can hear us and to pray to them. We are told how to pray, and it is to God.

There are demonic entities who pretend to be saints and other people we know. There are other entities who pretend to be a friend or a wise dead entity, but those entities do not know God's will for someone's life. It's for our own good that we don't communicate with the dead. We must know the Lord and read the Bible to know proper doctrine and to test the spirits. Otherwise, we can easily be led astray. The battle for the mind is real and strong. We are told to pray to God, not to people who have passed on to the spiritual realm.

> And when they say to you, "Inquire of the mediums and the necromancers who chirp and mutter," **should not a people inquire of their God? Should they inquire of the dead on behalf of the living**? To the teaching and to the testimony! If they will not speak according to this word, it is because they have no dawn. Isaiah 8:19-20 ESV [Emphasis Added]

> Now the Spirit expressly says that in later times some will **depart from the faith by devoting themselves to deceitful spirits and teachings of demons, through the insincerity of liars whose consciences are seared, who forbid marriage and require abstinence from foods that God created to be received with thanksgiving by those who believe and know the truth.** For everything created by God is good, and nothing is to be rejected if it is received with thanksgiving, for it is made holy by the word of God and prayer. 1 Timothy 4:1-5 ESV [Emphasis Added]

But, once we know Jesus Christ, we are delivered, complete, and protected from the evil one! Jesus Christ said:

> I have said these things to you, that in me you may have peace. In the world you will have tribulation. **But take heart; I have overcome the world.** John 16:33 ESV [Emphasis Added]